"dee's passions for the visceral stuff of life—food, cooking, love, running, loving, grieving—beckon us all to the table. Once gathered, her trailblazing life and reflections are set out in this chef-poet's characteristic precise and forthright prose. *Bread & Water* is a perfectly seasoned feast of a life in all its delicious courses." —JENNIFER COCKRALL-KING, author of *Food and the City* and winner of the 2017 Taste Canada Gold Award for Culinary Narratives

"The narrative strands in *Bread & Water* are braided together with a love that comes from a life of paying attention to the way food connects body to earth. Do your heart a favour and let it be charmed by this story of a big city food writer who moves back to the prairie and the leaky-roofed farmhouse of her childhood, reclaiming the family kitchen and the wood stove where she first baked apple turnovers with her grandmother. Hobsbawn-Smith will send you back to your own kitchen and garden, not merely to grow and prepare good food but to do it with care, gratitude, and love." —TREVOR HERRIOT, author of *Towards a Prairie Atonement*

"*Bread & Water* is not only a beautifully written collection of essays, but of a world (dee's world) opened up to us one page at a time. Her words are luminescent on the page, weaving together images and stories I won't soon forget. dee will take you down dusty country roads in Saskatchewan, to a cooking school in France, to a cramped Calgary restaurant kitchen, and no matter where you are, her words feel like home." —RENÉE KOHLMAN, author of *All the Sweet Things* and *Vegetables: A Love Story*

BREAD

WATER

Essays

dee Hobsbawn-Smith

University of Regina Press

Printed and bound in Canada at Friesens. The text of this book is printed on 100% post-consumer recycled paper with earth-friendly vegetable-based inks.

COVER ART: "Bread with water on a dark background" by vandame / AdobeStock

COVER AND BOOK DESIGN: Duncan Campbell, University of Regina Press
COPY EDITOR: Kendra Ward
PROOFREADER: Candida Hadley

Library and Archives Canada Cataloguing in Publication

TITLE: Bread & water : essays / dee Hobsbawn-Smith.

OTHER TITLES: Bread and water

NAMES: Hobsbawn-Smith, Dee, author.

SERIES: Digestions (Regina, Sask.) ; 4.

DESCRIPTION: Series statement: Digestions ; 4

IDENTIFIERS: Canadiana (print) 20210230037 | Canadiana (ebook) 20210230053 | ISBN 9780889778115 (softcover) | ISBN 9780889778221 (hardcover) | ISBN 9780889778238 (PDF) | ISBN 9780889778245 (EPUB)

SUBJECTS: LCGFT: Essays.

CLASSIFICATION: LCC PS8615.O23 B74 2021 | DDC C814/.6—dc23

10   9   8   7   6   5   4   3   2   1

University of Regina Press, University of Regina
Regina, Saskatchewan, Canada, S4S 0A2
TEL: (306) 585-4758 FAX: (306) 585-4699
WEB: www.uofrpress.ca

We acknowledge the support of the Canada Council for the Arts for our publishing program. We acknowledge the financial support of the Government of Canada. / Nous reconnaissons l'appui financier du gouvernement du Canada. This publication was made possible with support from Creative Saskatchewan's Book Publishing Production Grant Program.

This book is for my sons,
Darl and Dailyn,
and in memory of my dad,
W. Paul Smith,
and two friends,
Anita Stewart and Madeleine Kamman.

When I write of hunger, I am really writing about love and the hunger for it, and warmth and the love of it and the hunger for it . . . . There is food in the bowl, and more often than not, because of what honesty I have, there is nourishment in the heart, to feed the wilder, more insistent hungers.

—M.F.K. FISHER (1908–1992), *The Art of Eating: The Gastronomical Me* (Foreword, 1943)

CONTENTS

PREFACE

I t was 1983, and I was a young cook. My chef at the time was a purist who suffered bureaucrats and fools not at all, but he agreed to write to the provincial apprenticeship board when I asked him for a reference into the program. I'd attended a year-long cook-training program at a technical school in Vancouver, and had recently developed fluttering aspirations of cooking my way across Canada to end up in Montreal, the Canadian culinary mecca. The credibility implied by an apprenticeship would help. But I was still green, a beginner in a small but adventurous Calgary restaurant. I knew nothing of nouvelle cuisine, Paul Bocuse, or *les frères* Troisgros.

One day after my lunch shift ended, Chef put a fantastically small book into my hands. The author was M.F.K. Fisher.

"Read this," he said. "Then read *The Art of Eating*. Best food writer ever." He'd already made me read *The Auberge of the Flowering Hearth* by Roy Andries de Groot and *The Making of a Cook* by Madeleine Kamman, so I was willing to trust him; learning to cook with Kamman would change my life, as I have chronicled elsewhere.

I had no idea who M.F.K. Fisher was—an aged and revered American food writer and stylist by then only nine years away from her death. Unbeknownst to me at the time, the work of those two iconoclastic women—Fisher and Kamman—would plait up my life as securely as the strands in a French braid.

I read the little book, *A Cordiall Water*, with some amount of disbelief. Incantations and mystery? Ageless faith? The essentials of healing? Chef had called her a food writer, a narrow slot of classification that in my young mind began and ended with restaurant critiques. Then I read *Serve It Forth, Consider the Oyster*, and *How to Cook a Wolf*, the first three books contained in Fisher's five-book omnibus, *The Art of Eating*. By the time I finished I thought I knew the author—a witty, self-assured, erudite, and beautiful woman who lived, travelled, and ate well, and who had robust opinions on all three. I liked her style, as a woman and as a writer, so I collected her books, filling a shelf with them—essays, a novel and short stories, more food, including her *Time-Life* cookbook on provincial French food, autobiographical works, and two editions of her translation of Brillat-Savarin; then after her death, her collected letters and a few biographies of her. I was a busy young mother, chef, and writer: I promised myself to read them all later.

Four decades later, my restaurant career far behind me, I am close to completing a master's degree in Literature. My thesis focuses on Fisher's translation of Brillat-Savarin's 1825 classic, *The Physiology of Taste*. I should be reading D.H. Lawrence and Evelyn Waugh for my class, but today I plan to immerse myself all afternoon and evening in M.F.K. Fisher. It is a deliberate distraction: today we mark the first anniversary of my father's unexpected and sudden death.

None of us knew that Dad was two days from dying when an ambulance took him to St. Paul's Hospital in Saskatoon on a Friday evening in early October 2019. He was weaker than usual, scooting around the kitchen on his wheeled stool as he made supper, but Mom put it down to his arthritis—an obscure and painful form—giving him grief. Always an early adopter (at age eighty-three, his office was cluttered with techie toys he enjoyed mastering), he took CBD oil as soon as it was legalized, and an expensive experimental steroid, to manage his pain. He had become the house cook when my mom was bedridden after two simultaneous knee replacements. Dad's engineer's brain approached cooking as a spreadsheet, methodically eliminating one variable at a time in pursuit of a better dish. His experiments with ginger beef lasted weeks and used many pounds of meat as he tried the tough cuts first, finally settling on a quick-cooking bit of tenderloin as optimal before he tackled how to get a crispy coating without resorting to a deep fryer. He'd kept me updated, picking my brain for ideas and feedback, offering me taste-tests of what would become our lunch when I showed up for my regular Friday morning outings with Mom to the local farmers' market.

So today I am not rereading Fisher's early works. I have bypassed her lighthearted memoirs of meals in Switzerland and France with her first husband, Al Fisher, as, like my dad, she learned what worked. No. I'm reading the later chapters of *The Gastronomical Me*. These are sombre accounts of "sea changes"—train trips and voyages with her second husband, Dillwyn Parrish, known in her writing as Chexbres. It was the late 1930s and Europe was sliding inexorably, bleakly, into war. Chexbres had lost a leg to an untreatable illness and was facing certain amputation of his remaining limbs. He was dying, and they both knew it. They travelled to Switzerland to buy pain medication unavailable in the United States, deliberately existing in a short-lived bubble, determined only to love each other and live in the moment, the world illuminated and darkened by their awareness of the coming tragedies. Fisher's writing took on a clarity of vision, an unsparing, unadorned tone, as she recounted seeing German soldiers and Jewish refugees fleeing to Amsterdam. Then a political prisoner manacled to two Italian soldiers impaled himself on a broken train window; the train staff, who knew and loved Fisher and her husband from previous trips, did their best to shield them from the carnage. A year later Chexbres died offstage and off the page, among the trees outside their ranch home in California, shielding his wife from his suicide just as Fisher would shield her readers from his self-inflicted gunshot wound.

This writing—this is not the M.F.K. Fisher I thought I knew. This writing is grim but gripping: I can't set the book down all day. When I surface, a photograph of my dad as a young father floats into view. My last sight of him alive was in the hospital before and after surgery. Beforehand, the surgeon and I conferred outside of Dad's earshot where he lay in emergency, an oxygen mask over his face, Mom stroking Dad's arm.

"Exploratory surgery," the surgeon said. "He'll be in hospital for a considerable while afterward. He's very weak."

"But surely he'll be fine," I protested.

Then the unexpected. "He's facing a colostomy," the surgeon said bluntly.

I knew what that meant. "But my dad's too old! He'll never be able to cope with it."

"Do you want your dad to live?"

An hour later—so soon, I thought, surely that's a good thing?—the surgeon found us in the OR waiting room. He was flanked by two other people, and visibly rattled.

"You'll have to come to the OR to say goodbye to your husband, Mrs. Smith, to your father, dee. Quickly. We have him on oxygen to keep him breathing until you say goodbye."

Shock took a few minutes to percolate, but my ability to speak was immediately short-circuited. The surgeon patted my mother's arm as he explained that he'd found sepsis in all of my father's organs and inner body cavity. There was no miracle, no recovery. My father died within the hour as Mom and I held his hand.

Today, a year later, M.F.K. Fisher, the food writer who single-handedly defined the genre as the entire garden of life and death, accompanies me as I mourn. There's no more fitting homage to any writer of any genre or discipline. My dad, who had *The Art of Eating* on his bookshelf, would agree.

Dogpatch, west of Saskatoon, Saskatchewan,
7 October 2020

INTRODUCTION

Commonalities intrigue me—we all eat; we all need a home. Each of us has complex and evolving relationships with those realities. My own relationships with food and home are complicated by my former role as a chef and by my early gypsy life as the child of air force parents, with a further wrinkle added by the water of the title—flooding in two separate provinces. *Bread & Water: Essays* offers a meditative personal voice that bears witness and poses questions—even if no answers result. This collection of essays explores the quotidian in a search for larger meaning. I appreciate the irony that to describe the abstract, an essayist, like poets (and cooks), relies on the concrete.

I am indebted to the late American essayist M.F.K. Fisher for her poet's understanding of food as metaphor, which validates my continuing interest in food as a literary theme. "When I write of hunger, I am really writing about love and the hunger for it, and warmth and the love of it and the hunger for it," Fisher wrote in 1943. Then she goes on: "There is food in the bowl, and more often than not, because of what honesty

I have, there is nourishment in the heart, to feed the wilder, more insistent hungers."[1]

I have turned to writing about those wilder hungers that loiter beyond the hunger for love. In "Rapture" I consider the commonalities of Syrian refugees and Canadians through common tastes in food. "Ashes" explores the loss of a beloved dog within the context of digging ashes into a raspberry patch. In "Handmade" I think about my sons and their divergent kitchen paths; in "Watershed," "Floodplain," and "The Spiral Tunnels" I interrogate floods, place, and loss; "Prodigal" examines my return to an old home. "Learning to Cook" interweaves cooking methods with memories of my grandparents and my culinary mentor as I educate myself and my sons. In "Prairie Pragmatic" my political interest in local food weighs in against my grandparents' reality of subsisting on food they'd grown themselves, and in "Wiebo's Way" I look closely at my own life and parenting in response to a visit to a sustainable farm owned by a saboteur and his family. "Cooking with James" delves into the toxic world of male privilege in the restaurant world. "Surrender in Iambic Tetrameter" entwines my early equestrian ambitions, late-blooming running obsession, and the hungers that fuel both; and "Jobs That Taught Her More Than Cooking" peeks into some unusual professional kitchens.

Food matters. The COVID-19 pandemic laid bare the weaknesses in our global food production and distribution systems, and—in North America, at least—our systemic mistreatment of the immigrant and migrant workers who slaughter our animals and harvest our produce. We are more socially distanced than ever as restaurants—agents of culinary change, favourite gathering places, and community hubs—reduce operations and close. We have witnessed grocery-store shelves stripped bare of flour and yeast, and have returned to our gardens, home kitchens, and hearths in droves, driven by necessity.

As our bubbles narrow to include only a handful of our nearest and dearest, we are rediscovering the pleasures, meaning, and matter of cooking for one another and sharing meals. Now more than ever as the pandemic brings so many back to the kitchen, bread and water underpin my life. And yours, too. I'm glad to share.

LEARNING TO COOK

1. BAKING

> *To anyone who wishes to discover that there is much happiness and many opportunities for learning and becoming oneself in what is still considered by too many the least important room in a home or even in a restaurant, the humble and all-important kitchen.*[1]

My older sister, Lee, standing before our relatives and speaking the eulogy at our grandmother's funeral in the mid-winter of 2006, reminded them of how Gran's hands had helped shape what mine became. "My sister became a chef because of Gran," she said, pointing to where I sat in the front row of the small-town Saskatchewan church. Our family nodded soberly, Hutterites, never colony but still far too reserved to shout "hallelujah!" or to sing our grandmother into heaven. At age twelve I had briefly dabbled with a Baptist church, but each time I had rushed to testify or offer a harmony to the choir, I'd imagined my grandmother's quiet voice: "We just don't do things that way, Deneezie. Things take time."

≈

A kitchen is a place of change, of alchemy. Every cook is the magician who uses heat and time to transform a jumble of ingredients into something else, something other, a fusion of flavours and textures, removed from the original, greater than the beginnings. For three decades, conducting, observing, and recording those culinary transformations occupied much of my thinking, first as a chef, then as a writer. Each morning, I would stand at square one before my stove or my keyboard, hands poised. What to create today? Cooking is second nature to me now, but it wasn't always. My apprenticeship began in childhood. It was a slow, sometimes painful process.

≈

"When you can see through it, it's done," my grandmother said. I perched on a stool at the high counter, watching as she rolled strudel dough, thin, thin. She held it up, a parchment-like sheet draped over her wrists and fingers, and gestured for me to lay my palms on its surface. She shifted her square hands, the primal shape my own would grow into, so they mirrored mine, palm to palm, the membrane between us another fragile layer of skin that we coaxed toward transparency.

I was five in 1963. She was not yet fifty, but she seemed ancient to me, heavy and slow. The kitchen, hers then, is mine now; I am older now than she was then, but in my eyes, I'm younger, less exhausted by the physical demands of life, energized by—what, exactly? A better diet? A sense of purpose? But I can't claim to know that Gran had no sense of purpose: she was a farmer, and maybe that sufficed. We saw my grandparents only infrequently because my dad was in the air force, which meant we moved from base to base every couple of years; I didn't know either of them as well as I wish I had, but I've always realized that Gran was not the confiding sort. She would never have shared her doubts or her faith, and certainly not with a grandchild. I'm equally sure that she had questions about life; it seems an inevitable partner to aging. But I envy her faith. In its absence, I've turned to asking my own questions, and to wondering about the things she accepted as truths. But I do have one small truth—this kitchen still smells as it did in Gran's day, warmed by cinnamon and cloves, and the wood stove, occasionally smoking, the same stubborn flue.

That day in the kitchen, she bent close as we folded apples and dough into a ragged-edged packet, then brushed pastry with melted butter. Her apron grazed my back as I tugged the oven door open, her hands under my elbows as I slid the tray onto the rack. The enamel door of the oven was warm against my back as I sat on the floor. Then the long slow ticking-down of minutes, waiting for the oven to complete its miracle.

"It takes faith," she told me. "Ovens will do what ovens do." Then, "There's no hurrying, we just don't do that," she admonished when I fussed and wanted to pull things out "just to check, Gran, please!"

≈

It would be years later, in teaching my boys to make cookies, before I'd finally learn the lesson.

"Like this, Mom?" they would ask, spooning dough into uneven blobs on the tray, fingers smeared with sugar and butter. When the trays would emerge from the oven, their cookies would be all shapes and sizes, some crystalline lace, others baked into bullets. In those efforts, I would taste and see first-hand the myriad ways that dough can vary in each pair of hands, shape and texture influenced by time, temperature, mixing methods. The many ways sons are different from their mothers, and daughters from grandmothers. The many ways we face the inevitable necessity of surrender.

No hurrying an oven. No hurrying a grandmother. Some things rely on time passing. A red-tailed hawk lets the wind do the work as she hovers, wings open to the cross-current, and waits for the world to spin into alignment under her. A cook learns to let things be, to trust in the mystery of the kitchen. If that recipe for surrender could be translated so effortlessly to life, the cookbook would sell by the millions.

To a child in a hurry, the seconds sweep by slowly; for a mother looking back, the years passed too quickly. Those dawdling minutes, waiting impatiently with my grandmother in front of the farmhouse stove. Then the quick-quick, double-time burnt-before-you-know-it staccato timing of the sauté pan on the stovetop's cranked-up flame as my children grew up and left home. Time has no meaning in the kitchen. Time means everything in the kitchen. This, my grandmother knew.

2. KNIFE SKILLS

> *Take hold of the handle of the knife in your working hand (the right hand if you are right-handed or the left if you are left-handed); the tip of your thumb should rest on the ... corner of the blade where it joins with the handle. Resist the impulse to extend your index finger onto the blade; it may look chic, but it is unsafe.*[2]

Grampa spoke in guttural growls, English blended with Hutterisch, impossible to distinguish proper from profane.

Donnervetter! *Fahrflucht*! were some of his favourite curses. *Ne Messarnt* meant crop failure. *Trockenjahr*, drought year. *En Kjatel abgewürgt*, the tractor stalled. *Der verdammt Hund*, the damned dog.

Late in from the field, alone at the dinner table after the rest of us were long done eating, his face blackened by dust from combining and his elbows propped on the scarred wood, he used his knife to pick up pieces of meat from his plate. When he caught me looking at him from my spot on the steps, his blue eyes narrowed. Was he angry? I couldn't tell. At that moment he was a frightening stranger.

"Tomorrow, we butcher."

⇌

A knife case sewn for me by my father contains thirty knives, each blade safely encased in a scabbard to contain and protect its edge. But even sheathed, my favourite tools look like weapons. A visiting poet flinches when I pick up a sharpening steel and a French knife and slowly draw the blade, first one side and then the other, down the length of the steel—just so, honing the knife's edge into a razor against the steel's diamond core.

I try to reassure her: "Sharp knives are safer than dull knives." But I can see she doesn't believe me. I don't know how to tell her that a sharp knife cuts to the heart of things, exposing the core of what matters most. That dull knives are misdirections, prone to external pressures and mistakes. So I grab an onion and show her.

⇌

Next morning, recalling Grampa's words—had they been a warning?—I hid in the kitchen and ventured out only when my mother nodded to me as she stood at the mud room's metal sink. A slop pail stood at her feet. Her fingernails were rimmed with blood.

"You can go out and swing now. But stay out of the way."

The rope swing dangled at the far end of the garage, behind the tractor. I edged past the machinery, stopped, and stared into the recesses of the building. A light bulb blared overhead. Beneath it, a gutted steer slowly twirled on a hook, blood soaking into the ground, only the stain of salt left behind on the floor beside the heap that had been the animal's hide. The air smelled like hot metal. Grampa stood beside the carcass, the blackened carving knife he held reminding me of a scimitar I'd seen in a book of myths. Such calm in his face as he picked up his steel, drew the knife down its length, then down the steer's gullet. A precise line.

His voice precise, too. "Don't look away, Deneezie. This is your supper."

He filled big bowls with tidy pieces of meat, naming them. Tenderloin. Short ribs. Chuck. Flank. I made trip after trip to the kitchen, emptied the bowl onto the table, where Mom and Gran wrapped and labelled each piece, a year's worth of suppers. We'd take a boxful of frozen beef with us when we drove back to the airbase in northern Alberta.

≈

My sons each held a knife by age four. Soft fingers around a small black handle, a curved tip and serrated teeth the best insulation I could offer from the real bite that is a knife's job, careful of their tender hands in a way I never was with my own in my daily work as a chef.

"Put the tips of your thumb and index finger on the side of the blade just in front of the handle, to choke up, for more control. Like a baseball bat, remember, from the park?"

An onion, rolling on the block. "It wriggles around, Mom! How can I make it stay still?"

"Tuck your fingertips way high up and arch your hand like a cat stretching, like this. The blade goes under the bridge your hand makes—and now the onion falls in half. A flat surface, see? Now lay down the half on its flat side."

A carrot, its long tail pointing toward soup. "A rocking motion, honey. The knife moves, not the carrot."

Then a rack of lamb, the boning knife so like a pirate's dagger. How could I deliberately put such a dangerous tool into my children's hands? They were still too young to understand if I told them a knife could cut a path to self-reliance, just as hard times could expose our dullness and grind out our flaws. That if we were lucky, what remained would be lucent and hard-edged, steeling us for the decades to come. No. I could only show them my faith in them. Don't look away, Deneezie.

3. BUTTERFLYING

> *Place the piece . . . on a cutting board, the fattiest side down. Cut 1½ inches deep into the meat lengthwise, then cut 1½ inches deep across the meat to the left at the bottom of the existing cut. Now cut 1½ inches deep across the meat to the right. Open the piece of meat on the board and smooth it with the flat side of a chef's blade knife.*[3]

"Madame, I am here too early in my career. I don't know enough."

"Nonsense, *ma belle*." Madame snapped her fingers. "This is why you are here. To learn. You are never too old or too young to learn. Being twenty-six is not a problem. You will store this knowledge like a seed. When you are ready, it will germinate. Tell me, why are you frightened?"

The year was 1985. I was the youngest of six students in
Madeleine Kamman's cooking school in Annecy, in the French
district of Haute-Savoie. With my husband and my infant son,
still nursing, I'd flown to Europe, then driven from Amsterdam through France to the mountains. At the French border,
when customs officials had queried me about the contents of
the cooler in our camper-van, I'd struggled for the right phrase,
then finally shrugged like a true francophone. "*Les groceries*,"
I'd said in my English-Canadian accent, and they'd smiled.
Every morning, I left son and husband at the businessmen's
hotel where the businessmen drinking coffee in the café invariably frowned at us, and dashed through Annecy-le-Vieux and
across the bridge to Madame's kitchen classroom. Each night I
would return long after dark to wake our child and hold him to
my leaking breasts with relief.

Long before Toronto restaurateur Jen Agg called out male
chefs on social media, berating a toxic anti-woman work environment, Madeleine Kamman, the kitchen's Iron Lady, was on
the mark and flying the feminist flag. In the 1970s, she turned
a photograph of Paul Bocuse, the famous French chef, upside
down in her five-star Boston restaurant because he'd said that
women did not belong in the kitchen but in bed. Her third
book, *When French Women Cook,* first published in 1975, was
dedicated to the millions of women who do cook. In the introduction, she wrote: "Where are you, my France, where women
cooked, where the stars in cooking did not go to men anxious
for publicity but to women with worn hands stained by vegetables peeled . . . ."[4]

I was one of a small handful of women cooks in Calgary
in the 1980s. When the first chef to oversee my apprenticeship, an anti-establishment contrarian, suggested I needed to
gird my loins, he had the good sense to suggest Madame as
the ideal bolsterer. She was a fierce martinet, a hawk teaching

her professional younglings to fly to Michelin stars. Writing in the *New York Times*, food writer Molly O'Neill later called her "a purist with an encyclopaedic knowledge of food chemistry and food history, and a harsh judge . . . the superego of modern America."[5] Madame was more than just a chef capable of accurately writing a recipe that would guide a novice through reproducing a classic French dish. To the many chefs she inspired, Madame Kamman taught the soul's culinary terroir—respect for place, history, method, ingredient. She did it in the kitchen, hands-on with her students, not by retreating to a television studio while an audience sat, inactive, passive, and not cooking (although she, like Julia Child, did eventually star in a series of televised cooking-show classes, albeit for PBS).

She was to be my mentor, my idol, my embodiment of the war goddess Kali, and she would terrify me for decades: assisting Madame at a cooking class in Calgary ten years later, I would bounce into the kitchen, humming some pop tune, calling loud greetings. Madame would look up from the counter, the Brandenburg Concerto smoothing the air around her. "You cannot simply barge into a work space, Deneezie," she'd say coldly. "Show respect, if you please."

That mid-eighties summer in France, as part of our education with Madame, we visited markets, farmers, and producers, sowing the seeds of my locavore beliefs. At each stop, Madame would scrutinize the goods on offer, her nose crinkling as she assessed—and only sometimes bought—before we returned to her kitchen. There, we discussed what we had seen and tasted, planned a menu, and always, cooked.

One morning we visited a mountain *fromagerie* east of Annecy, high in the Alps of the Haute-Savoie, where the local cheese, *reblochon*, was made with the second milking of each day while the cows grazed the nearby summer pastures. The second milking was the original tax dodge, Madame later explained: medieval farmers paid *l'ociège*, or taxes, on the volume of milk their cows produced in a day. So the farmer would milk the cows lightly in the morning, then—after the morning's amount had been recorded—milk again late in the day, without declaring the second milking's yield, less abundant but richer and quickly made into non-taxable cheese.

"A washed rind *fromage du fermier, et lait cru*," Madame said, pointing to the wooden racks covered with rounds of cheese, each in velvety orange-yellow jacketing. She sliced a wheel open and sniffed it, then handed out a plateful of ivory wedges, admonishing, "You will find it nutty and herbal. *On ne mange que la crème.*"

"What did she say?" one of the Americans whispered to me.

"Farmhouse cheese, raw milk. One eats only the cream."

The class made pilgrimages to Michelin-starred restaurants—across Lake Annecy to Auberge du Père Bise in Talloires; by bus over the Swiss border to Crissier, to dine at Girardet; and to Lyon, to Bocuse, his past insult overlooked—meeting chefs whose names appeared in newspapers, whose cooking had reshaped cuisine. On those days, Madame's eyes raked our North American apparel with disdain. "You intend to eat at Bocuse in *that*?" she hissed one morning, smoothing the fit of her Chanel suit as we congregated in cotton skirts and sandals. "You people. You have no sense of style. Just as with food."

After the market on those mornings we were not travelling to dine, we gathered at Madame's kitchen counter over brioche and *café crème* to critique the previous day's efforts. Then Madame allocated the day's dishes: "Tracy, *la truite amande*; Sally, *tarte au citron*. Martha, *les haricots verts* and *le pain fougasse*. Deneezie, today you cook the protein. *Le veau.* Stuffed as we discussed. You know how to butterfly it, yes?"

Beside me, my American colleagues calmly unpacked their knives, not a sheet of paper in sight. I hunted frantically for relevant recipes in my slim stack of cookbooks lugged the long trek from Calgary. *My knife is too dull. I will never master this.*

I was sweating, swathed in an ankle-length apron. Madame glared through her wire-rimmed glasses. At me. Again.

Staring down at four hundred francs' worth of veal loin, I started to shake when my knife slipped down its spine. A ragged hole appeared in the meat. Madame was at my side within moments. Sniffing.

"Did you not learn how to butterfly a piece of meat at your Canadian school? This—this—is not well done. You must caress it, like a lover, not hack at it." She plucked my knife from my fingers. In her palm, the knife became a wand. She placed it on the veal and gestured, a magician's sleight of hand. "So." The veal acquiesced, opening in one continuous sheet, thin and pliable as parchment. The knife landed on the maple butcher block with a dull thud.

I should know this already. French cooks begin their apprenticeship at sixteen.

"*Encore.*" She retrieved my knife, placed the grip between the fingers of my left hand. "Practise, *ma belle.*" She twitched her fingers, and Joanne, her assistant, appeared with another veal loin. "To begin, technique is all. Your hands will know soon enough. Then—only then!—we discuss flavour principles. Until then, use your knife. And taste. Taste everything."

4. SAUCE-MAKING

> *Perhaps in no other culinary preparation is corner cutting more dangerous than in sauce preparation, be it the most refined of French sauces or in the most fragrant and well-balanced of Indian chutneys. Trust your intelligence and palate . . . .* [6]

Sundays, before I retreat upstairs to my studio to write, I spend two hours in the kitchen. The stovetop fills with pans. Flames flicker and flare, the ancient incantation. The stock pot simmers, bones releasing proteins, gelatinous and rich. Lamb braises with yogurt and garam masala; lentils shimmer in a pool of turmeric-yellow stock, the air heavy with ginger, garlic, cumin. Madame's voice in my ears—"Triple *tombage, s'il vous plaît*"—as the stock undergoes multiple reductions, its water level falling and replenished repeatedly, as she'd insisted. Strained, the stock gone caramelized amber, it reduces into a sauce, bubbles breaking on the surface, embodying "a steady reduction," as O'Neill wrote, "a process of purification and distillation."[7] Lessening does not diminish. This comforts me as my years left to live diminish. The end result—after, and because of, my own repeated falls of many sorts—might yet be a clear, concentrated life, distilled to essence.

≈

My fifty-first birthday. Both my sons arrived at my yellow *boîte* of a house a block from Calgary's Bow River. They jostled each other, laughing, shouldering like good-natured colts in a paddock. My small kitchen seemed smaller than usual; their voices and bodies filled all the spaces that normally folded around my ribs like close-fitting feathers lining a nest.

"Hey, Mom, where's the roasting pan?"

"Pass me the colander, bro. How am I supposed to drain this pot with you standing right in front of the sink?"

"Did you reduce the stock for the jus? Who's going to make the Béarnaise sauce?"

They made a festival out of the moment.

≈

I am writing at my desk upstairs in our Saskatchewan farm-house when the phone rings; I know it is one of my boys. Both are capable cooks, and both work in restaurants, the elder in the kitchen, the younger front-of-house, their apprenticeships unwinding like an apple peeling to the core of what they need to learn.

Dailyn: "Mom, I'm at home canning peaches. What can I add to the syrup that will taste yummy?"

A day later, Darl: "Mom, that Korean flank steak marinade. Can I add horseradish or wasabi, or do I have to use sriracha?"

I don't miss the irony that I second-guessed my sons' choices of career when each gravitated to restaurant work. This, despite my own life in the kitchen. "Have another calling in your hip pocket for when you hit forty," I've told them. "Cooking won't last."

But I see their open hearts. And I have learned: my fears are mine alone, fed by distance, age, time.

Of course cooking feeds them; they saw from childhood how it fed their mother. Cooking does last. People have always needed cooks; it is a noble profession, the dance of flame on metal. We all eat, although not all of us cook. What I really meant to say was that their bodies, perfect now, the Adonis bodies of active and healthy young men, will eventually wear down beneath the weight and stress of the restaurant world. But just their bodies. Never the inner flame.

WATERSHED

Dave and I arrive in Saskatchewan in July 2010 on a sweltering hot day. We arrive to dryland dust as the uninvited guest at every meal, to darkness so thick it wraps us like a duvet, to the scent of sage and wolf willows, to sunlight that slants across wide summer skies, leaving shadows of owls and coyotes in its wake.

The excitement that buoyed me through packing the house in Calgary slowly deflates. What comes in its place is that long evening light and the delicate English rose of early-morning sunshine. Their fragile peace is upended by a ragged battalion of barn cats bounding to greet me. Behind them trails my parents' farm dog, Amigo, a Great Pyrenees who'd never adapt to town life and is left behind to guard us. Will this suffice until I find my footing?

I left Calgary to help my parents as they age. And to live a slower life myself. Ironic, that, as I also leave behind my food writing career, where I wrote often about Slow Food and its global calling to change our lives and attitudes. But mostly I

left Calgary to pursue my dream of writing poems, essays, nov-
els, short stories.

I bring my cat and dog, but leave my sons behind, both
full-grown. Is it selfish to leave? No. Engrossed in their own
burgeoning lives, they'll miss me less than I'll miss them.

But on arriving at the farm where my grandparents had
lived, I realize that my loss is eased in part by my newly found
sense of belonging, something I never felt in Calgary. Here, the
feeling is bolstered by *them*—my ancestors, the invisible ones
who silently move the door ajar. We are surrounded by ghosts,
but they are benign. We sleep in a room my parents slept in,
the air initially heavy with a sense of trespass. We live under a
blanketing swathe of stars I don't recognize, so many I can only
marvel. We are surrounded by rutted country lanes—without
street signs or lights—that at night could lead anywhere, or
nowhere.

A week after we arrive, the rains begin.

≈

My grandparents lived here for thirty years, amid animals,
grain fields, greying barn boards, garden. It rarely rained.
The only water for miles stood stagnant in occasional
sloughs and the dugout, or hid down the well. On mid-sum-
mer visits when I was a small girl, walking to the pumphouse
for water, my grandmother and I swung buckets between us
on smooth wooden handles. The buckets' white metal was
carved russet by oxidation, the metal thinned like membranes before childbirth. She wore equanimity as her robe,
corseted with the implacable gaze of the stars that oversaw
her long country life.

Each afternoon, I scrambled into the old green Mercury
with her to check the mail, the air inside the car hot and heavy,

dust infiltrating at each window and gathering on the dash and cushions. She sat tall at the wheel of a grand limousine as we cruised past the barn and along the verge of the field and up the driveway lined with aspens and poplars.

"You jump out and check the mailbox for me, *Liebling*, I'm just an old lady." Her deep voice was soft and rounded, patient vowels like the butter she slathered on my corn. I carried the newspaper and the mysterious sealed envelopes into the farm kitchen. Its walls were yellow, slatted cupboards from floor to ceiling. A wood-burning stove hulked by the north wall. In its reservoir, iron-red water. As an adult, I paint every kitchen yellow.

≈

My father is not a farmer by birth. At thirty-six, in 1973, he and Mom packed us and our pets away from the Fraser Valley to the farm where Mom had been raised. New to farms, he adopted his father-in-law's protective colouring. Soon he cursed the overheated pickup truck, tumbled-down hay bales too loosely stacked, failed crops, worse weather, Wheat Board policy, the price of grain. Nearly forty years of prairie winds haven't smoothed his edges. Has he ever loved living here? He is so quick to let go: a month after Dave and I arrive in 2010, Dad tells me, "If you hadn't taken up residence in this house, you know what its fate was to be, don't you?" The unsaid: demolition. The house hears. It never welcomed him; he only perched on its outer skin. Years later, my father would elaborate: "A tractor would've pushed that old house into its foundations if you hadn't come back."

I'd been fifteen when we arrived in '73. And I was glad to shake off that pervasive dust three years later when I moved to Vancouver, where, years later, in 1981, I'd go to cooking school.

≈

Dust is a rural prairie constant and reminds me of the wind that always lurks behind the trees, a wind that seems non-existent most of the time to town dwellers. When Dave and I move in, I wipe dust from every surface, scrub the house's bones and gunnels, squelch my dismay at mouse droppings, keep from wincing at my tired parents' leavings. This is our house now. It's sturdy, the core of it over a century old, a mishmash of unplanned rooms assembled by need. Will it become home? I run rust-tinted water into buckets, clean walls until the aging lath and plaster glows, wash windows, polish counters, vacuum every corner, collect abandoned clutter entangled in the caraganas that frame the yard, haul away trash in the truck I never thought I'd own—a pickup, rusting too.

As kids, visiting at school-year's end, we had summer barbecues in the south pasture beside the dugout. While Mom cooked weenies on a stick, the five of us—my siblings and me—ran through hazy air in pursuit of gauzy dragonflies. Poplar branches were dryads leaning in to the fire, a bucket of water at hand to douse any sparks in their hair. I sat beside Gran as she roasted marshmallows, watched her pass Grampa the perfect one with a hidden molten heart, its toasted-sugar crust trumping the heavy scent of wolf willows.

In their wedding portrait, taken in 1936, my grandfather's wavy dark hair is so slick, so strictly under control, betraying no hint of his fierce temper or his bitter Hutterisch curse words that heated the air around him when the farm resisted his will. Beside him, no higher than his shoulder, Gran radiates composure. Her round face looks placid beneath crimped hair, a small fur stole around her neck. My mother is already a bump beneath Gran's belly, concealed by hands folded in her lap. Too much like my grandfather, I yearn for Gran's grace, that restraint. She looks so like my calm elder sister, it's as if her ghost walked through the frame.

⇗

Writing is why we came here. I write as if the well has opened to me, an artesian spring pouring water cool and clear and clean into my hands. For the first two months, I observe Dave's silent keyboard and wonder if he is now my muse, if his ray of inspiration has glanced its way from his aging body to my younger one. What is fair among the gods of artists? Where do they cast their gifts, and for how long? I dare not say anything but blessings, even as I observe his silence. To my relief, the silence cracks apart one day and the air fills with the clatter of his keyboard and the jazz he loves to listen to while he writes.

The house calls. Finally I give in and leave my desk. I unpack books, kitchen tools, winter clothing. The move-in work seems endless. There are no closets in this old house: in the early days, our people had used wardrobes, and my mother followed suit. As will I. Unpacking photos of my sons brings on a flood. I wonder if this is a fool's dream and cry again. Gazing beyond the house, my eyes stumble over rows of old things: machines and cars; grey dilapidated out-buildings— the barns, two garages, bunkhouse, greenhouse, several small storage sheds. Every building and field is crammed with broken and corroding evidence of three generations, stuff left by those thrifty souls who believed "everything has a second day, keep everything." Can I live in the shadow of the past without losing my own momentum?

Vibrations send out a whir audible through windows. I sense, then hear, the hummingbirds, and scurry to refill the feeder hanging in the blue spruce, a bellwether of my longing to come face to face with flying magic. The hummers hover, survey, navigate the tree. They pause before plunging needle beaks into each spout of the feeder, one after another, tasting for different meads. Finally they settle tiny wire feet on the ring and halt their wings. It is restful to hear the silence—such stillness in a plainsong-chanting landscape.

The spruce raises its head above the south row of caraganas. Ralph Waldo Emerson ostensibly said, "The wonder of it is that we can see these trees and not wonder more." This tree survived decades without watering, growing as gnarly as my grandfather. It's impossible to visualize him as young and straight—to me, he was always old, always hunched and bent, but burly, his former strength still palpable. Mom tells me he got only a grade four education before he had to go to work as a hired hand—his father died young in 1911, in suspicious circumstances, leaving a widow and seven kids. How would Grampa's life have changed if he and this landscape had been watered?

On a late August afternoon in the early 1960s, hoping to avoid the endless drive and being jammed into the stuffy car elbow-to-elbow with my brothers—hours of discomfort that would carry us back home to the airbase northeast of Edmonton—I tunnelled into the abandoned dog house behind the blue spruce, hoping to hide until after the family left. I came out screaming, wasps in a cloud behind me. My grandfather's long arms plucked me from their swarm. So quietly, he brought a dipper full of water as I lay on the bed's patchwork quilt. The air of the bedroom was as cool as his hands and the calamine lotion on my angry skin. My grandparents are the reason I am here.

≈

It is ironic that things are not simpler, not auto-idyllic, in a rural setting. This old house and its land throw curve balls, all garbed in the simplicity of nature's primal forms. At each mention of the well, cranky with its century of service, anxiety closes my throat. Water flows out, yes, but water so hard it gives me a bellyache, water I hated to drink as a child, water loaded with minerals that erode metal like etchings and leave behind evidence of the transformation. "When you install a hot water heater here," my father tells me soon after our arrival, "within five years, it quadruples its weight."

I imagine particles from faraway planets, or remnants from the ice age. In the sand hills a half-mile from our yard, sand breaks down into its constituents and infuses itself into this hard water. I am swallowing corrosive glass, my gut says, with each mouthful of water drawn from beneath the hills. So we compromise—wash with well water, haul drinking water from town. Still hauling water, like my Gran had in the years before pipes ran water to her house. Another irony.

But eerie lights flash whenever the well's pump runs. The pump-house window, looking east toward our house, is illuminated by pulsating Morse code; then the light takes a long-drawn breath and holds it, a lighthouse beam that does not exhale or dim. One night, out looking for our cat, I notice the steady glow. My anxiety bursts full-blown at the sight. What does it mean?

One Saturday afternoon in August, anticipating my parents' arrival for dinner, I fillet the steelhead, wash the knife. The water tap slows to a trickle. Near panic, I close the valve, steeling myself. Tentatively, I try again half an hour later: a dribble, then air. In desperation, Dave and I open the notebook labelled *Farm Life for Beginners* that my mother left behind for us, and we reread everything she recorded about the pump. In her sloping handwriting and oblique wording, there is no urgency, no explanation, just a too-brief list: *check about re-airing pump; watch the light; check the power; ask your father.*

I pick up the phone and make another call to home base, feeling helpless, childhood revisited yet again.

My mother is offhand. "The light in the pump-house? It should come on briefly, maybe for twenty seconds at most whenever the pump runs."

Or. The hanging unspoken conjunction. Or what? Then what happens? She's vague when I ask. I want to shake the notebook, the phone, loosen the dangling threat of *maybe* into reality. Listening to her, I am discomfited to realize that my unease about the light is grounded in a real issue. When will I learn to trust my gut?

That evening, after we grill and consume the steelhead, my father launches another "Father Knows Best" lecture on what I should have known: the pump was signalling its distress, but we couldn't interpret the signals. I follow him to the pump house, where he works some arcane magic on the pump, magic he can't or won't explain. "There," he says. "That should do it. For now."

Back across the yard at his heels, feeling like a chided pup. In the kitchen, he opens the tap and red water gushes out. In less than a year, we will replace both pump and well, and my anxiety will subside.

≈

Rain falls throughout August and into September, and becomes a torrent, swamping the driveway. Such volume is unusual here, where desert-verge dryness is the norm. Road and rain both run through what is now a slough, our neighbours' cattle up to their hocks in water and grass and muck, thick as gumbo. But when I walk out in my rubber boots, it amazes me—how quickly the breezes dry the sand on the verge, how I kick up dust, and a few metres away, wade through mud that threatens to steal my gumboots from my bare feet.

One eye to the sky, we hurry to harvest the tomatoes. Sixty pounds lie in cloth-lined baskets, the occasional sunset flare among mostly green orbs. But they've received too much moisture and bloom into blossom-end rot. Just a few pounds are salvageable.

A red-tailed hawk glides above the stubble during yoga one morning, the same slow ballet, lazy wings barely moving. I flutter my arms and try to emulate the hawk's grace. Behind her, weather rolls in from the northwest, greyness tall against the horizon and moving with purpose. No more rain, please. We are almost locked in by that long mud-plagued road, held hostage to the weather. I foresee a day when we will be isolated here, unable to drive out, our neighbours our lifeline— maybe this winter, if the snowplough can't carve through frost-hardened windrows, or perhaps next spring, if the mud and water rise in an impassable mire.

The roof on the house is a lamination accrued over time: first, black tarpaper; then wood shingles; then a seventies-era layer of cedar shakes was added by my dad—still accustomed to West Coast house structures—without an additional shield of tarpaper in between. With this downpour, leaks ensue. Raindrops ping and plop on unaccustomed surfaces. Soon buckets stand in the basement by the furnace, on the main floor beside the wood stove, upstairs in a row along the windows like offerings to the Buddha. All my words are placed on hold while I mop up errant splashes. Is a roof's purpose to keep things out? Or to keep things within? How does a writer find what lies within when the roof leaks? Maybe it's a double blessing in disguise. I want my grandmother's optimism to outweigh any potential for disaster.

The rain stops. The roof dries. I clamber onto its spine, the cat deft beside me, curious about my venture into his domain. Tiptoeing and sliding along the steep slope, I finally settle on my butt for best balance and pound loosened and errant shingles back into place with the business end of a fencing tool. My addition is lumpy, beginner-ish, but if it works I will be redeemed. A new roof, yet another layer, but metal this time, with its own problems, will be added four years after our arrival, and all the cedar shingles will be stripped off and saved for kindling.

Climbing the stairs into my studio a few days later, I step into light like stained glass embellished with vines, all spun from rose and silver: sunrise, coming through the east window and the hops' trellis, the sun cradled farther south each morning. Fall is coming, cool, cooler, cold. In the kitchen one early morning, I read six degrees on the thermometer. Quick! Set kindling alight in the wood stove, haul firewood from the basement! The steps so steep, narrow, no guardrail. Cement crumbles into dust on the wall beside my outstretched hand, contradicting three inches of water standing on a dirt floor.

≈

The ground ices over into near-winter, residual water sparkling into gems that crack beneath my boots when I cross the low spot just south of the house. Red willows blossom with hoarfrost, fairy dust sprinkled and frozen. Marvelling at their intricacy, I turn the corner behind the greenhouse to find stiffened carrot corpses, scrubbed and forgotten. Nothing in city life prepared me for the tough sensibility of this unforgiving landscape. Then the spuds, Yukon Golds and russets planted by my mother in the spring and so painstakingly dug: later that afternoon, I unbuckle the woodshed door and find them, coffined in brown bags, their inner moisture crystallized.

Bone-deep, the cold settles in, its early arrival shocking, but a relief from rain. The road is striped wide-wale corduroy, rutted and deep but drivable, the mud immobilized by frost. We buy an insulated water bowl for Amigo and Mojo, another for the barn cats, and keep the tap water running on the coldest nights to prevent freeze-up in the septic tank. From prosaic to picturesque without missing a beat, the true nature of rural life. Yesterday was a leaden glass day, all pewter. Today's stained glass sunrise has dissolved into crystal, blue and silver.

By afternoon, the sky turns heavy, no light breaking through. Wind howls from the east, snow pending. I feel it waiting and retreat to the sunroom, hover by the window, listen to the singing of Dave's reborn keyboard, and work hard to recall what it is that I like. The red sun rising. Three deer scudding across the south pasture through the hay bales. Cattle congregating contentedly. Big sky. Chickadees, snug in their little black bonnets. Words that sort themselves into a resonant voice. The flutter and spin of the aurora borealis across that belt of star-studded sky.

The bird feeders empty. Snow falls. We wake to white silence. The fields and driveway close their jaws on more snow than is imaginable. To open the gap, I study the dictionary, first looking up the obvious. *Snow*, and all its descendants: *Snow angel. Snowball. Snowbank. Snowboard. Snowbound. Snowfall. Snow fence, fort, goose, leopard, pea. Snow shovel. Snowslide -storm -suit.* At *snow tire*, our neighbour Ken's tractor with the plough-blade bolted to its nose growls up our driveway. My mother has informed me that cinnamon buns are his preferred mode of payment. I bake extra for the next storm.

All these tribulations. The cold. How did my Hutterite ancestors survive when they moved to the district from the Dakotas in the early 1900s, with none of the amenities we now take for granted in our soft urban lives? And how did my grand-parents manage on this farm, from the late 1940s through to the early 1970s, with two young daughters, three rooms, no run-ning water, and power they used only sparingly after its arrival in the early fifties? My grandmother's calm demeanour, my grandfather's simmering anger—these masked their underly-ing hardiness, a rough-hewn robustness verging on stoicism in her, and damped-down dynamite in him. The admiration I feel for them is tempered by amazement, and my brief moment of self-congratulation for taking on this rural life crumbles and disappears. In the years to come, my mother will recount sto-ries of her childhood and youth, their lives then, and I will serve as her willing amanuensis.

≈

The longest winter, ice to its core, finally comes to an end. My keyboard has woven the weft and woof of something new, more words waiting to fill the pattern I don't yet recognize. I lay down the work to its rest and drive away to visit my sons in Calgary as the calendar turns to April, an early spring and early melt. On the phone the day before my return to Saskatchewan, Dave is mysterious, telling me to not attempt the driveway, but without giving me any reasons. I envision mud. When I return, I park at the end of the driveway beside the road and stare. Our shallow saucer of land, the lowest in the district, cups the neighbours' runoff as well as our own. Water stretches in all directions, surrounds the aspens, laps at the fenceline. A lake, and me its lady.

The lake's riches are for me to excavate, silt, sift, sort. A line from Saskatoon poet Elizabeth Philips' poem "Before" flashes into my head: *I'm going to say it now, / are you listening? You can only get there / by water.*[1]

I see Dave beyond a flood of snowmelt, waving. He straddles an all-terrain vehicle, not a fairy sledge, prosaic but still magical. I clamber up behind him, the snow geese crying overhead.

"We're flooded, baby," he says, "life's an adventure," and takes me home.

COOKING
FOR JAMES

Vancouver's streets were slick and wet, the pavement disappearing under iridescent puddles, the sky closing in on a Saturday afternoon in September 1982. I was avoiding my cooking school homework, soaking in Kitsilano's shabby-chic ambiance, shop after shop blurring like their reflections in the puddles as I idled along West 4th Avenue on my bike. When I stepped through the door of the kitchenware store, the room was redolent of garlic and damp wool; the aisles, crowded. All faces were turned to the chef behind the stove.

James Barber was already famous in Vancouver. His raspy voice had become familiar to Canadians over the CBC's radio airwaves, first as culinary tutor to Don Harron and then, more recently, to Peter Gzowski, on *Morningside*. But within the decade, James would become a global figure. Following TV culinary pioneers like Julia Child and Graham Kerr, *The Urban Peasant*—as James called himself—would broaden the horizons and palates of his audience while championing simple, local cooking.

I took the last seat in the store's small demonstration area, marvelling at how James made everything seem so easy and straightforward as he chatted and chopped his way through a brunch menu. When he finished cooking, I joined the snail-like queue to meet him, clutching my courage like a wrinkled apron. Finally face-to-face, I tripped over my words but somehow remembered to tell him I was a culinary student, then surprised myself by spontaneously inviting him to dinner that evening.

When he raised his eyebrows and inquired, "What will you be making?" I blurted out a lie.

In as airy a tone as I could muster, I said, "Oh, you know, crepes."

But I hadn't planned to make crepes. For months, as a newly minted vegetarian, I'd been investigating Indian food, entranced by the layers of flavour and colour as beguiling as Indian women's clothing, those flowing pants and tunics called salwar and kameez. As a preface to each meal, I grated ginger; pounded galangal, coriander, and fennel; and dry-roasted and ground cumin. I was slowly learning how to build subtle curries and refreshing raitas and spicy chapatis—all messy but delicious and worlds away from the restrained roast beef, pork chops, and mashed spuds of my childhood. For my supper that evening, I'd planned on simmering carrots in coconut milk with Indian spices, then grilling a few chapatis in my black cast-iron pan to mop up the juices. But crepes were French. Surely they had more cachet than curry, especially to this man about the world. A contradiction was buried there, between James's fondness for simplicity and my sense that he'd like something more nuanced than curried carrots, but I didn't see it then, and Indian food did not yet have much culinary currency.

James had been raised on his English mother's dreary overcooked stodge, then discovered the wonders of peasant food while he served as a corporal in the Royal Air Force, gathering military intelligence in France during the Second World War. French country folk served him simple stews, lip-smacking roasts, succulent vegetable gratins, and crusty breads, all made with inexpensive, locally grown ingredients. Their textures and robust flavours astounded the young Englishman. In Vancouver, he created a patchwork career as a theatre critic, restaurant reviewer, and cookbook author before venturing onto the radio. There, James served up a potent homebrew of slightly *outré* French food and uncomplicated English pub-grub leavened with humour, a hint of sex, and an uncomplicated pleasure in cooking and eating. He somehow managed to bypass what would emerge as the curse of cooking shows: an audience glued to its chairs in the living room, not in the kitchen cooking.

"Hmmm," James said to me, turning back to the young woman who was waiting for an autograph. "And will you be cooking anything else?" Each word was Dover gravel on a patch of Old Country lawn, his teeth like a white picket fence. I'd only seen photos of him, and his forehead was more pronounced in person, his receding hair more tonsure-like, his laugh lines deeper, his nose more obviously pug. He was not as attractive as he'd seemed in those stills, but he still possessed a magnetically devilish smile that made me *want* something I'd never had: glamour.

I was a naive twenty-something, insecure as all young people are, with no faith in my own judgment or the impartial judgment of my mirror. Looking down at my muscular cyclist's thighs, I was convinced of their unappealing breadth; looking at my nose in my mirror, all I saw was its pronounced bridge. I was plain. And I was lonely. I'd grown up in a large family, cooking bland prairie fare for a tribe, sharing a bedroom with my sister, jostling for my share of everything from space to second helpings. When I'd arrived in Vancouver straight out of high school to discover coastal cuisine and enroll in culinary studies, I'd settled into a bachelor apartment and a string of unsuccessful affairs, latching on to whomever looked at me twice. Learning how to be a grownup was harder than I had imagined.

"Crepes," I said again, feeling that familiar desperation as James Barber stood behind the counter, clicking his pen and winking at the young woman, who'd taken back his book with slow hands. I didn't even like crepes. Their flabby texture made me think of a chapati that had failed at achieving selfhood. "And dessert crepes, too," I added, "filled with chocolate."

"All right then," James mumbled as he signed a book from the stack the store clerk had thrust at him. I scrambled in my backpack to find a scrap of paper, wrote down my address and his arrival time—seven o'clock—almost kowtowing as I put the paper in his hand.

James would go on to write an impressive number of best-selling books to keep pace with his TV show, but he already had a reputation for prodigious and varied appetites. On my frantic pedal toward home, I tried to remember what else I had said to him during our brief encounter. Something about hoping I'd become as quick-thinking a cook. Liking his food. Appreciating his uncomplicated and casual style, his unabashed use of whipping cream and butter. A fan's inane blatherings. Why couldn't I have said what I meant without sounding like a total geek, opinion-less, and innocuous as a day-old quiche? And why had I said I'd make crepes?

We'd made crepes two months earlier in class, shortly after I'd read James's offhanded account of making crepes Suzette in his first book, *Ginger Tea Makes Friends*. At school, my first attempt had torn when I tried to flip it, the tender batter overwhelmed by hands that had not yet learned grace or subtlety.

Chef René Jolicoeur, the head of the hot kitchen, had shaken his head, his immaculate apron lifting like a bellows across his rotund belly as he sighed.

"Slow down, *Mademoiselle*. I keep telling you: the world is not a race." He ladled melted butter, then batter, into the hot pan, swirled with a flick of his wrist, and set the pan on the flame. "Now, you wait. So. And now . . . you flip." Another graceful motion, too quick to analyze, and the crepe lifted in a slow parabola and fell back into the pan. He watched me make a mess of another attempt, then pursed his lips and shrugged, that Gallic multipurpose self-absolution. "*Encore une fois, Mademoiselle*. I require of you six crepes before class finishes today." I had persevered, but the bell sounded before I could show Chef any more than two, both flawed.

≈

It was still raining when I locked my bike outside the liquor store. Inside, I agonized for twenty minutes, knowing I was about to spend most of my month's grocery budget. I finally sprang for a famously expensive French white burgundy I'd never felt quite up to trying before, intimidated not only by its hefty price tag, but also by its reputation and high score with the wine experts, unconvinced my student palate would do it justice. But those attributes—and its provenance—seemed perfectly aligned with tonight's endeavour.

The wall clock read three when I manoeuvred my bike through the building's awkward entry and jammed it into the narrow hall of my tiny apartment. I found the crepes recipe in my class binder and clutched it in one hand as I pulled ingredients from the fridge with the other, then groaned. I was out of eggs. The clock's hour hand was a spur, and my nerves were already wound tight.

The trip back to 4th Avenue and the health food store took just a few minutes, but the lineup at the only open cashier's till was the normal weekend logjam. The woman in front of me had two whining kids, a cart full of frozen soy-cheese pizzas, mini-yogurts by the case, and a dozen school-sized bottles of juice. I saw her eyeing my carton of eggs, perched alone on the conveyor belt, but then she looked away and concentrated on picking lint off the hood of her daughter's rain jacket. I vowed again never to have kids, to concentrate on my career and become a famous chef, to give all my change to panhandlers, to let people cut in front of me at the video store and at the grocery store with impunity and a gracious smile.

"Will there be anything else?" the cashier asked when my turn finally came.

I hesitated, then snagged a handful of chocolate bars and flung them on the conveyor belt.

"Can you wait just a sec?" I asked. I bolted to the back cooler and grabbed the last glass pint bottle of whipping cream. "I'm cooking a French dinner," I said to the scowling clerk when I returned. "Crepes."

"That'll be fifteen dollars and fifty cents."

"What? For eggs and cream?"

"Organic eggs. And that's Avalon Dairy whipping cream. Six bars of dark Ghirardelli chocolate. Fifteen—"

"All right, I got it." I counted out coins and tightly folded bills sequestered in my wallet. The last of my food allowance and my month's bus fare, as well.

The batter looked flawless. The cream sauce bubbled on the back burner, waiting for the carrots to be sautéed in butter. But my imagination kept intervening, smearing James's pen-and-ink drawings from his cookbook into a bizarre live-action cartoon. "Crepe filling," I heard him say in that gruff tiger's purr, "is a vehicle for improvisation. Make a cream sauce, fry some sliced asparagus, add diced chicken or smoked trout. Snazzy. Sexy. Simple." In my mind, he invited a young blonde who looked a lot like me onto a stage set up as a kitchen—similar to the store earlier that day, and to the television set when he'd host *The Urban Peasant* several years later—and grinning, he fed her enormous mouthfuls, cream dripping down the fork to his cuff.

Peeling and slicing carrots in a frenzy, all I could think about was the look of pleasure on the real James's face as he ate my crepes. As the carrots softened in a bed of butter on the stove, I picked up four chocolate bars, smashed them down on the counter, pulled off the wrappers, and dropped the broken bits into a small pot with the rest of the cream—chocolate ganache for the dessert crepes.

On the radio, John Cougar was singing "Jack and Diane." The whole world was caught up in love, infatuated with the idea of coupledom, wheels spinning in tandem. Cooks had the inside track—James Barber's success proved that people invariably let down their guard while enjoying a yummy meal cooked for them. Tonight, I was boarding the train.

I made a fresh pot of coffee, lit the front burner, tossed a knob of butter in my pan, attempted that insouciant swirling motion I had so envied, added the batter, and swirled again.

The batter didn't swirl.

It set, in jagged arms and indentations like the inlets along the Georgia Strait. I tried to loosen it, recalling Chef's admonitions—that the pan had to ready itself, that the first crepe was invariably spoiled, to make enough batter to account for loss. *To account for loss.* I was only twenty-three, but I'd been struck by the phrase, wondered if it extended to people, to families, to children, to pets. To careers. How to plan your life with sufficient resources to account for loss? Who would want to?

I tried again. Failed again. I added more milk and tried again. The third crepe broke as I flipped it. The fourth landed on the floor, as did the fifth. Ten minutes later, I was sweating, my pulse up again, my coffee pot empty, my hands shaking like a junkie's. Of twelve crepes that eventually made it onto the plate, six were worth using. Six were sufficient. Maybe. I knew my guest's reputation, his famous appetite. I recharged the coffee pot, refilled my mug, and set to work tidying up.

An hour later, I laid four crepes in a baking dish, stuffed them with the cooled carrots, poured on the sauce, turned on the oven, and spooned the chocolate ganache into the remaining crepes, my pleasure at the finished result attenuated by increasing anxiety. I paced the hardwood floor of my apartment, looking out the window every five minutes, trying to see through the dim twilight. I could hear raindrops pounding on the glass, water cascading down the cracked sill.

By seven, the doorbell hadn't yet rung. When I opened the fridge, the French burgundy waiting all alone in its depths convinced me I had earned the first glass. Survivor's due. Forty minutes later, the wine was half gone. By eight thirty, my blood sugar plummeting, a headache creeping up, I put the carrot crepes into the oven then ate the last of the chocolate cream sauce, dipping salvaged pieces of crepe into the pot like a penitent before the grail.

I pulled the crepes out of the oven half an hour later and topped off my glass. The clock read nine thirty, then ten. At ten thirty, I finally ate the meal I'd prepared, alone, sitting on the floor with the television on, my plate of soggy crepes balanced on my lap, wine glass on the floorboards beside me.

I barely slept that night. At school, I didn't mention the fiasco, although I did tell Chef I'd successfully made crepes.

≈

A month later, I was at my stove before class, radio blaring for company, and I heard James's growling baritone interrupt Gzowski's voice: "Nothing is as seductive as cassoulet." I imagined him stirring a pot of cannellini beans and crooking his finger at an attractive brunette working the soundboard in the radio studio.

You fraud, I thought.

I added ginger and cumin to my lentils, and turned off the radio before I ate.

≈

The crepe incident haunted me for years. I mostly blamed myself, although, in my thirties and by then living in Calgary, as I struggled to raise my sons while running my restaurant, I thought of James as a lecher. Then, in my forties, after I'd sold my restaurant, I reinvented myself as a successful and ever-curious newspaper food columnist—much as James himself had done. At first, I wrote about culinary celebrities and chefs, then graduated to advocating for local ingredients and sustainable food production. In 2001, I encountered James again when he came to town, his latest book in hand, to teach two classes at the city's leading gourmet cooking school. He didn't remember that we'd met previously, when I was still green, and I refrained from telling him directly that he'd stood me up, but I made light of the fact in my column. He hadn't changed: life was still a series of seductions, and over noodles and barbecued pork in my favourite Vietnamese joint, he told stories of his fondness for women and of his long courtship of one in particular.

During our conversation, wildly paraphrasing a quote often attributed to the poet Rainer Maria Rilke, James said, "Passion is more than four legs in a bed." (Rilke had written about marriage, not passion.) Then he ascribed the aphorism to the English lexicographer and writer Samuel Johnson—a comment and attribution he would use more than once in conversations with journalists. "I fall in love regularly," he went on, "with the sunshine, a colour, an ingredient, a philosophy. And I am desperately in love with ankles." Laughing—and blithely ignoring the double-barreled insult he was dishing out—he told me how he'd taught "a Virgo woman to make love to a risotto" in the previous evening's class. "It was the ultimate seduction, cooking in front of all those people. She'll never forget that. Food is always about seduction."

Later, considering things over a cup of tea in my kitchen, I bludgeoned myself with the enduring conviction that back in Vancouver, I'd been a plain young woman with little to attract a potential lover. A few minutes later, tea cooling in the cup, I changed tack and reiterated my suspicion that nothing I might have cooked two decades ago would have been sufficiently uptown to draw the urban peasant to my door.

≈

The simple fare of the urban peasant and his old-school attitude toward women in the kitchen were only precursors of what was yet to come. The Food Network launched into the kitchens of the world in 1993. Within a few years, New Orleans chef Emeril Lagasse was shouting, "BAM!" on TV screens across the continent. A little more than a decade later, competitors on *Chopped* were battling for supremacy in kitchens designed as war zones, complete with sabotage.

By 2002, Anthony Bourdain, an irreverent New Yorker with attitude and a taste for the world, had inherited James Barber's "sexy bad-boy chef" title, taking TV viewers into global markets and restaurants with sardonic good humour. Bourdain spoke openly about his double-edged rap as a recovering drug addict who suffered from depression, and his untimely suicide in mid-2018 left a large gap in the world.

On the plus side, though, before his death, and partly as penance for how he had glorified the professional kitchen's "cowboy" culture in his book *Kitchen Confidential*, Bourdain— who by then had a daughter—played a role in exposing and hopefully ending the trade's pervasive men-first/women-last, "bros before hoes" ethos. He wasn't the only foodie keeping pace with the zeitgeist of the #MeToo movement: high-profile Toronto restaurateur and author Jen Agg has been loudly calling out abusive male chefs—in public, in newspaper essays, on her Twitter feed, and in her book, *I Hear She's a Real Bitch*.

Agg is a rarity, though, as are the women chefs working in restaurant and hotel kitchens. In the early 1980s, when I was a culinary student, less than 25 percent of students enrolled in the Vancouver Vocational Institute's cooking program were women. In 2016, the Culinary Institute of America in New York enrolled more than 50 percent women. But a depressingly low number of women stick with it, only to toil in professional kitchens as prep cooks, line cooks, and sous-chefs, with only a few reaching the summit as chefs and restaurateurs. Why? Agg and Bourdain had the right of it, and TV's portrayal of women chefs like Nigella Lawson or Rachael Ray as sizzling and sexy hearth goddesses doesn't help. Things haven't changed so much since James's time, after all.

But it's simplistic to blame TV. Those ubiquitous screens are symptoms of our collective losses, not causes. Food and cooking are complicated snapshots of our culture. Longer work hours, the outsourcing of jobs in our work-world, and the rise of the single-parent family, coupled with fundamental changes in how we view food and its production—as a commodity, as cheap fuel, and as an overworked and underpaid trade practised by largely invisible hands, in stark contrast to the star-chef culture—has led to perhaps-predictable results.

On top of that, merely *watching* chefs cook on TV does not teach a captive audience the textures and smells and experience of actually cooking. Radio, with its room for the imagination to play, was better. Regardless, too many modern diners prefer to eat out or order in instead of tying on an apron. (A nod here to the global resurgence of home cooking as a result of the pandemic. I hope the habit sticks.) That passivity means that home cooking is a dying skill and, with it, significant familial connectedness; when we give up control of our stoves, we surrender the stove and kitchen table as fulcrums for conversation and debate. On that score, James, who made his bones teaching people how easy it is to cook good food, would be appalled.

≈

When I heard the news of James's death in 2007, I sat down to take stock of his influence, a glass of Riesling and a bowl of lamb curry in front of me. I wish it were as simple as saying James taught me to view cooking as something to enjoy, as something worth sharing, but my feelings of gratitude and loss were overlaid by my resentment of how women continue to cope with the morass of male approbation and disapproval. At nearly fifty, I was single, with a broken marriage behind me, and I had two almost-grown sons who embodied the grace and appetites of athletes. I'd taught my sons to cook and watched them go through the same uncertainty I felt at that age. I'd owned a restaurant, written cookbooks, fed other chefs, served food to possible partners, and learned how to mop up my heart when the prospective dates didn't take root. And, despite my old chef-instructor's warning, it never occurred to me to plan for loss. It always seemed self-defeating to me, as if it were too risky to bet on success or happiness. Risk is a necessary ingredient in a fully lived life. That, I learned from James.

Even after my years as a chef and restaurateur, I prefer to turn up the flame and write the menu fresh every morning. I've let go of believing I was a failure because James didn't come for supper. I unhesitatingly invite strangers to dine; there's always room for another chair. I only serve dishes that flutter my heart, and I still swoon for a good curry.

JOBS THAT TAUGHT
HER MORE THAN
COOKING

1. THE JOBS SHE DIDN'T GET, VANCOUVER, 1982

A pattern for a Chanel-style tailored skirt and cropped jacket with Nehru collar. Raw silk the colour of heavy cream, piped and lined with ecru satin. She spent a week cutting and stitching, hours after class bent over her Elna. One day the suit was finished. She put it on with a yellow silk blouse and a pair of flats, then hit the streets, filling in job applications at a dozen good restaurants. She wore the suit to the college one day after a tour of Beach and Denman, where she'd papered the desks of every good chef in the district with her sparse resumé. She was halfway hopeful about the famous Italian trattoria, but only because the school had sent her there for two days to prep vegetables; and the woman chef at the fish house had looked more alertly at her application papers than had any of the other chefs. But none had asked her to return for an interview.

She met her classmates in the cafeteria, where they were lounging over coffee before they changed into their whites.

"You look like a wee fairy princess," Gerry, the Cape Bretoner, said in his slanted brogue. "Or a daffodil. Where you been, then, darlin'?"

She confessed she'd been job hunting.

"In that?" He shook his head in disbelief. "You don't look strong enough to throw pots around a kitchen in that charmin' wee suit, darlin'. They'll stick you on the hostess station out front for sure if you show up for an interview looking like a fashion queenie. You want a cooking job, you need to look like a real trap-smasher."

Later that day, one of her instructors—the tall Dutch pastry chef who'd worked the Indonesian cruise ships in Southeast Asia, who cooked the students lunches of nasi goreng and "killer rice" loaded with fiery bird's-eye chilies and sweet *kecap manis*—grilled her on why she was in cooking school.

"Why don't you go to university instead and get a nice job as a dietician?"

"Because I want to be a chef!" As he turned away, she saw the eye roll, the smirk, the shoulder tilt as he shrugged.

≈

In late October as their year of classes concluded, Gerry told her he'd successfully applied to the kitchen crew of an oil and gas company doing exploration in the Arctic Circle.

"Give it a shot, darlin'," he said. "You of all people should be able to find a job in half a shake. You smoked us all in class."

"Just in the theory section," she corrected him.

"The practical skills come quick. You'll catch on in no time."

She sent off her letter of inquiry, cautiously signing it with her initials and surname, and was elated to receive a response—addressed to Mr. Smith—asking for her particulars. Two weeks later, a second letter bearing the Arctic company's logo dropped through her mail slot: *Dear Miss Smith, thank you for your application. All our positions are currently filled.*

2. SCOTCH BOTTLE ON THE TV, FERNIE, 1982

Her first employer picked her up at the Cranbrook airport in pea-soup fog, drove her through the labyrinth of mountain valleys without conversation. Wordlessly he showed her around the motel's kitchen. A middle-aged baker in a chocolate-smeared apron impassively made pie dough at the counter behind the freezer. A thirty-ish blonde woman in tight jeans, her whites half-buttoned with lace showing at the neckline, stood at the pass taking order chits from a server wearing a ruffled red apron. "That's Barb," the owner said, nodding at the cook. A freckled salad girl with purple hair hanging in her eyes washed iceberg lettuce in a stainless sink big enough to drown a St. Bernard puppy. A tattooed dishwasher was being harangued by a line cook who brandished several pots. "Meet your new chef," the owner said to them. Their names flew past as he introduced each.

"Here's the walk-in," the owner said as they entered a fridge the size of an up-ended coffin. "It's a tight ship, so keep it organized. You can start tomorrow. The Greyhounds arrive at ten and four en route to Vancouver and Calgary. Take a look around, familiarize yourself. Barb can help. Give me your produce and meat orders, I'll call 'em in. All daily specials to me by eleven. That's eleven tonight." He dropped a key in her hand. "Your room is on the ground floor at the back."

She'd found the job among the postings on the bulletin board at the college when cooking school ended. "Sure, you're ready!" her favourite chef-instructor had said, his ink-line eyebrows raising unasked questions on his puckish face. "But the mountains? Are you sure? I could call a couple chefs here on the coast. No? Had enough of Vancouver, have you?" She hadn't admitted that she was leaving a lover, not the city. But even as she'd called the motel in the Kootenays to arrange a phone interview, the turmoil in her gut had told her what she already knew—she wasn't ready to run a kitchen.

≈

Next morning at ten, a Greyhound disgorged fifty passengers at the motel's front door. The bus driver strolled up to the café's counter where she stood in her whites, watching the customers fill the booths, dismay rising in her like a flood of cold seawater.

"Forty minutes till we roll out," he said, brushing invisible lint from his grey jacket. "That coffee fresh?"

Servers filled her hands with orders and ran away. Barb, her platinum hair tied in an elaborate knot atop her head, came over and took the scraps of paper.

"I'll call the bills," she said. "Maybe you should take the grill?"

For the next half-hour, she heard Barb's voice calling from the pass while she dropped baskets of French fries and chicken fingers and onion rings into hot oil, turned steaks and burgers and pork chops on the grill. Sweat dripped into her eyes, blinding, stinging.

Everyone got fed. At the end of the shift, Barb patted her on the shoulder. "You'll figure it out."

She didn't figure any of it out. Cold on the spot of ten and four, the room filled, the bus parked like a ghostly mastodon outside the motel. Bills dropped from her fingers, from the rail, from her awareness. Each shift was a laser lightshow of confusion that quickly became chaos, servers huddling on the other side of the pass, line cooks mistiming burgers and steaks, salads going missing, her boss standing in the doorway, arms folded, watching as the diners waited and waited, bus driver tapping his foot at the counter. The bus left late, irate passengers hurriedly cramming burgers into mouths and wrapping unfinished slices of pie in napkins. Was this why she'd endured a year of cooking school? To be a short-order cook? What about her dreams of white-tablecloth cooking in Montreal? Travelling? *Stages* in Europe?

≈

One afternoon after a clusterfuck of a morning—produce truck and their week's order lost in the ditch along the ice-slick mountain highway from Calgary, salad girl's hand sliced open by a carelessly placed knife, baker uncharacteristically burning three raisin custard pies and slamming out of her kitchen corner in wrath—the orders in her clutching fingers suddenly shuffled into a poker hand in her head, seven-card draw, aces high, nothing wild. With authority, she clipped them on the rail in front of her as she called each one, rapid-fire, a dealer at a high-stakes game.

"Ordering, three steaks, all medium-well, kill 'em, three house salads, no fries. Ordering, two burgers, loaded. Ordering to go, one chicken club on rye, naked Caesar, dressing on the side, no croutons, no cheese. Ordering—" And later, "Pick up, table two. Pick up, counter. Pick up, table six." The hour flew by. She glanced up once to meet Barb's eyes. The older woman nodded before slinging her dirty pans into a bus pan for the dishwasher. The driver at the counter grinned and tapped one finger to the brim of his hat in salute as he shepherded his flock to the bus.

≈

The steep mountain walls encasing the valley closed in as winter hit the solstice. The sun's arc shortened to six hours of sunlight. Someone stole the extension cord protruding from her old VW's block heater. A bottle of Johnnie Walker Red Label took up residence on top of her television in her motel room, the level dropping with her spirits. No one to talk to.

≈

Her parents drove through winter glare and arrived on Boxing Day, shook hands suspiciously with the owner after eating in the café with the uprooted and the holiday road warriors. Turkey she'd roasted with stuffing, frozen green beans, iceberg wedges and Thousand Island, and the baker's best chocolate pie after the mincemeat sold out.

"Let's go for a stroll," said her father back in her cluttered room, eyeing the Scotch bottle. They walked through Fernie's frozen narrowness as the afternoon dropped its curtain, her mother wordlessly snapping photographs. Years later, in the family album, she'd see a snapshot of herself and her father with grey mountains closing in behind them, labelled in her mother's sloping script: "Most boring day in the known universe, Fernie."

≈

Two weeks. Three. She twisted up her courage like an apron. "I can't do this," she said to the motel owner.

"I know." He pursed his lips, gauging her. "I'll pay you half of what I promised."

She said goodbye to Barb and drove up the hill to the new ski lodge. Chef looked her up and down. Jeans. Boots. Not a silk suit in sight.

"Can you make a nice Béarnaise?"

She nodded.

"Show me."

She got a job as first cook in the dining room, making Béarnaise and Bordelaise, boning quail no one ordered, cutting and grilling tenderloin and T-bones and lamb chops. Dinners were slow: most diners, still wearing their skiwear from the hill, preferred the coffee shop or the bar *après-ski*. The Scotch bottle took up residence on top of the TV in the apartment she shared with three waitresses from the hotel bar, all of them just out of high school. On days off, one of them taught her to ski. The Scotch bottle emptied. In the evenings after her shift ended she propped her elbows on the counter of the lodge's bar and drank Glenfiddich neat, falling into bed too drunk to succumb to the temptation of calling her former lover in Vancouver and begging to be taken back. He would, she knew it— her departure had been her own idea. She woke one morning with a hangover and no recollection of driving home from the ski hill. Stumbled out into the frozen fog in a fugue of terror to examine the VW's bumper. In case.

Chef quit and went to Vancouver. The irony didn't escape her.

Three months. One day she realized she needed more than a town in a mountain valley. She left the valley and moved to Calgary.

She arrived in Cowtown just as the National Energy Program hit. Businesses locked their doors. Signs cursing the federal Liberals and Prime Minister Pierre Trudeau hung in vacant office towers that had housed oil-and-gas head offices.

3. LA NOUVELLE CUISINE, CALGARY, 1983

The help-wanted ad included words like *nouvelle cuisine* and *fresh sheet*—not the Calgary-carnivore norm. At the bookstore she found the only book on the shelves with nouvelle cuisine in its title, read it from front to back, memorized new tenets like laws from the mountaintop. *Modernist. Reduced-fat. Sauces by reduction.*

The interview was terse. "What do you know about nouvelle?" the chef asked. He was narrow and dark-eyed, a Celt with bristling manners.

She rattled off her newly acquired tenets, salted with newly learned chefs' names—Frédy Girardet, Michel Guérard, Paul Bocuse, Alain Senderens.

He raised his eyebrows. "How would you construct a modernist Béarnaise sauce without using egg yolks and melted butter, but that still carries the original flavours?"

She squeezed her memory, desperately trying to solve the puzzle, but none of the recipes she'd stuffed into her head from the book fit the bill.

"Never mind," he said. "Are you willing to learn?" At her sheepish nod, he grinned. "Good. Smart cooks are scarce as hens' teeth in this godforsaken town. Now put away that damn book you crammed from and I'll teach you a few new things about cooking."

He kept his word. She learned to think on her feet, to use what was in season and on hand, to make sauces without starch, to achieve pure and intense flavours. He hired other smart cooks, as well. They became friends, bonding over shared work lists, scribbled recipes, tornado lunch rushes that left them flattened, evening doldrums when diners stayed home in droves, afternoon espresso, late-night wine and tunes in her basement suite, dim sum on days off. She bought books by other chefs, including a tome on methodology by a Frenchwoman, Madeleine Kamman. "She's a tiger," said her chef. "A genius. You should go study with her in France. You'd learn more from her than your damned apprenticeship program."

She met a man. They later married. Her unexpected pregnancy coincided with a required stint at school for her apprenticeship.

"You'll come back?" the dark-tempered chef and the owner both asked. She shook her head, already sure that learning came from forward movement.

4. LOBSTER ON A BIKE, CALGARY, 1984

She stumbled across the inner-city warehouse joint by accident, a loading dock out front, a too-busy down-at-heels bar across the street with dealers clustered at the door. The café's owner dredged oysters in cornmeal, fried them and added hot sauce, then called them Jamaican, shouted across the warehouse to greet his favourite customers. She taught the servers how to make cappuccino. Shucked oysters by the dozen, made Cobb salad with crabmeat, steamed clams with sausage, simmered chowder thick with potatoes and cod. Lunches were crazy busy. Dinners non-existent.

She worked for cash. After several months, he sent her home. Just handed her the envelope and a lobster, still kicking. "Thanks, see you around. Good luck with the kid."

She put the lobster in her backpack and biked home, heavily pregnant, her weight a bit tippy on the ten-speed. Teary but resigned. At home, after her husband named the lobster Robbie, she couldn't throw it into the boiling pot. Her husband winked, shook the lobster at her, tossed it in the pot.

5. ALONG RESTAURANT ROW, CALGARY, 1987

"My secret weapon," her boss called her whenever a visitor came upstairs to where they sat knee to knee, perusing foodie magazines and cookbooks at a tiny table in the owner's office overlooking 4th Street. She'd been hired to work on R&D, testing new menu items.

The place was unlike any restaurant she'd ever worked in, a small city of industry hidden inside three renovated houses: no chef, just kitchen managers; regimented recipes in varying batch sizes in binders; sales projections based on day of week, time of day, weather; a sunshine-dependent patio; morning "par" counts of line fridges and salad table and walk-in contents by kitchen managers; similar counts by bar managers; an army of hostesses, servers, bartenders, line cooks, prep cooks; an accountant, an office manager. And a resident dog, a golden retriever taken for a walk each day by the office staff. The owner, a tall, striking blonde woman with cheekbones sharp enough to slice paper and dark eyes that missed nothing, had come from an IT company. She lived by standardization and systems. And her, the R&D chef, neither fish nor fowl, answering directly to the owner, winding through the labyrinth past all the smiling staff to find her spot in the back kitchen, or climbing several staircases to the upstairs office to sit at the tiny table. "Little Chef," one of the kitchen managers—a giant Teuton who towered over her—called her, but respectfully.

≈

November. The Winter Olympics were coming to town in several months. Her boss wanted to open a high-end general store with house-made goods to cash in on the influx of hungry visitors. She tested recipes in the back prep kitchen, measuring, timing, scribbling notes, repeating with variables, reporting weekly. The winners became daily specials. A few made it onto the permanent menu.

Not everything worked out. Her boss made that sour off-centre face at her one morning as she reported on yet another depressing failure with the fudge she was struggling to fine-tune. "Depression Fudge, let's call it," her boss quipped.

That winter, her in-laws planned a Caribbean holiday at Christmas for the five of them—the baby was a toddler by then. Afraid of those eyes and the slicing cheeks, she didn't know how to ask her boss for time off. When she finally brought it up, her boss said no, she was needed here to get the general store tuned up.

A week later, she gathered up her nerve. "I'm going to Barbados—the tickets are bought and paid for."

Her boss stood up, visibly angry. "Pack up your knives. Don't come back."

She went. Barbados was warm but she was haunted. She came home to a notice saying her boss had denied her severance pay and blocked her application for benefits. After a painful arbitration hearing, the panel described the situation as one of terrible communication on both sides before awarding her severance and benefits.

6. SNAKE ON THE MENU ("DOES IT REALLY TASTE LIKE CHICKEN?"), CALGARY, 1988

Seriously? And alligator. How adventurous was too adventurous? She quickly realized that some creatures never assume the distancing mantle of "edible foodstuff." Once a week, she cleaned and portioned alligator for Chef, a Russian émigré who braised the lean slabs in lemongrass and ginger miso broth. During service, all she needed to do was reheat a portion, but the image of tooth-infested jaws shook her composure. The snake, however—a sinewy coiled rope, chewy and surprisingly bland, filled with toothpick-bones—bit her professional pride the deepest. She couldn't get past a mental image of swarms of snakelings escaping a nest each time an infrequent order crossed the counter.

One spring evening just after the Flames had been knocked out of their playoff run, the dining room held only a few guests. A server reported that a tableful of stockbrokers with Flames jerseys over their suits were loudly daring each other to order snake as they drank round after round of caipirinhas.

Five orders of snake hit the grill. She left the line as soon as they were plated. When she emerged after puking in the bathroom, Chef was waiting at the pass.

"Get tough," Chef said. "You used to ride horse, you say. How if I put horse on the menu like French chefs? How you handle this?"

She turned white as a sheet. Lasted two months as sous-chef.

7. UPENDED IN DOWNTOWN, CALGARY, 1988

She took the downtown job as executive chef in a historic building. It felt crowded from the get-go. She had three line cooks, a prep cook, baker, salad girl, two dish washers, and three bosses—a mother and her sons. The restaurant shared space with two theatres and the symphony.

"Dinner starts early on symphony and theatre nights, a three-course set menu, in and out fast," one of her bosses—the elder son, the nicest of them—had said at the interview. "They come back for dessert and drinks. If the show's any good." She'd nodded and grinned, told him she'd worked as a short-order cook in a mountain town with a Greyhound passing through it twice a day. Never thought she'd ever be able to joke about that, or claim it as an asset.

Her new menu got good reviews. The cooks, old hands, already knew how to cope with theatre crowds. A few months later, she learned she was pregnant with Baby the Second. Her fast hands and creativity and polite demeanour faltered. Fatigue came calling.

The youngest boss had early on made a habit of rolling into the kitchen with a chip on his shoulder. "Chef," he'd say mockingly to her. Never anything more. But she felt his disdain. When he learned of her pregnancy, he bowed with a flourish, smirking.

One evening during the post-theatre dessert rush, the dessert and salad fridge died. The salad girl, muttering, shifted its contents into the temperamental backup fridge at the rear of the kitchen, jammed next to the dish pit. Next morning, the fridge was still out.

The youngest boss strolled in just as the lunch orders began to roll in. At his greeting, she looked up from her handful of chits. "When will the fridge be fixed?"

"Chef. In the walk-in. Now." His voice was a saw grinding through metal. In the walk-in, he glared at her. "It's customary to greet the boss when he arrives."

"If I wanted to kowtow and grovel, I'd be down on the street working the stroll with the other girls," she snapped.

It escalated. His voice could be heard outside the cooler. "Pack up your knives and go home, Chef."

At home, she wondered if she'd been fired. Never considered apologizing.

Boss Number One—the mother—called that evening. "You *will* be in tomorrow, won't you?" It wasn't quite an apology, but it was close enough.

At six months, she bowed out. Earlier than she'd planned. "We'll have your job waiting for you after your mat leave," the three said, nodding in unison. Like those wind-blown lawn ornaments, she thought.

She went home to have her baby, knowing she'd not return. Swore she'd never work in another restaurant unless she owned it. Kept her promise.

PRAIRIE PRAGMATIC

When the first interviews for *The 100-Mile Diet* aired on the CBC in 2007, my mother called me, laughing. "Don't those BC writers know that some of us have been eating locally all of our lives?" she asked. My mother was born near the dryland Saskatchewan farm that Dave and I would eventually move to in 2010. By 2007, Mom had lived on that farm for over thirty years with my dad after an air force life spent on the road. While raising five kids, she'd kept a garden wherever we lived, always finding ways to stay close to the earth: as a young woman in Comox, on Vancouver Island, she worked as a field boss at a truck garden; a decade later, in the Fraser Valley, she turned her hand to local vegetable processing, taking a job in the cannery just down the road from the fields where hop vines reeked of beer-to-be.

I never questioned my mother's ethos, or our diet: not until 2007 would the *Oxford Dictionary* unveil *locavore* as the word of the year, but like my mom, I had been living by its still-unwritten tenets for decades. As a young woman I studied cooking with Madame Madeleine Kamman in France in 1985, and we routinely went to market each morning—where Madame minutely examined locally raised berries, cheeses, vegetables—before writing that afternoon's menu; and in 1992, my Calgary restaurant, Foodsmith, was one of the city's first restaurants to feature and name local producers on its menu. Then in 1993, I met Canadian cuisine queen Anita Stewart, who forced me to reassess my ideas when she insisted that Canadian cooks look beyond lemons and vanilla beans to what grows within our own borders. By 2007, my home pantry bulged with foods gained through my relationships with the local growers I wrote about in my weekly newspaper column. I was already convinced of the benefits of a local diet, so the pump was primed for the debate that followed: Was a year-round local diet viable only in Lotus Land, where apples fell not far from the tree? Or could it still be done—as my grandparents and parents had—on the prairies, as well? Still living in Alberta then, I set myself a challenge: how far through the year could I eat local prairie-grown fare? But in chronicling a year of my Alberta-first diet, I wasn't talking "fancy-panties" dinner parties, merely everyday cooking. I still had a teenager at home, and he ate every two hours. Where would urban coastal idealism and rural prairie pragmatism share common ground?

≈

At my desk, I designed a makeshift compass with a pencil, straight pin, and silk embroidery floss. On the maps hanging on my office walls, I used the compass to inscribe a series of concentric circles with my house at the centre. Innermost was my own garden. Locally raised vegetables, meats, and regional cheeses were the next ring, then fruits, vinegars, and wines from BC's valleys, a day's drive away. The fourth ring added the broader national foodshed of wild-caught BC salmon and hal-ibut and Dungeness crab, Québécois cheeses, Saskatchewan wild rice, and Nova Scotian scallops and lobster. On the exterior grew the international garden of coffee, chocolate, olive oil, citrus. I resolved to use as little as possible of those goods that travelled the furthest.

My assumptions: I would eat well; I would shop locally first, as I always had; I would make few compromises in the process; I would continue to cook from scratch.

My questions: What were my breaking points? What could and could not be found in Alberta's backyard? How well would I eat?

Inspired by my friend Jeremy's English-style front-yard "allotment" garden, I began planning a new vegetable bed—leeks, lettuces, arugula, beets, carrots—to take root beside my sour cherry trees. Then I said farewell to my favourite spices—cumin, cinnamon, cardamom, cloves, the warm tones of the Middle East and India. I'd be relying on my herb garden's hardy Euro and Mediterranean flavours—basil, thyme, tarragon, dill, oregano, rosemary, coriander—fresh from my planters, or from stocks I'd dried and put by as my grandmother had.

≈

So. My first meal. Breakfast seemed a likely candidate for smooth seas on the good ship local, but it gave my first taste of heavy weather: coffee. No coffee plantations anywhere in Alberta. Seven in the morning, day one, and I was already making my first exception. How many would there be? In a world of concentric ripples, coffee beans might as well come from the outer rings of Saturn. Then, as now, I love good coffee, and self-denial had neither virtue nor a spot on the breakfast table. But even in the dirty thirties, my prairie-born farm grandparents had purchased coffee beans! So while I stood in my tiny farm-style kitchen close to Calgary's Bow River and contemplated glass jars of beans, grains, dried mushrooms, and flours, I held a full espresso cup.

While I stood in thought, my youngest son staggered into the kitchen, still semi-somnolent. I'd warned him that I'd stricken citrus, bananas, and peanut butter from the shopping list, so he wordlessly poured himself a glass of black currant juice, guaranteed to scrub any oxidation from the brain. He made a smoothie of homemade yogurt and frozen berries and departed for work. In the silence of his wake, I plopped the remains of the yogurt in a bowl and topped it with granola and an afterthought of jam.

My work as a freelance writer mostly kept me at home. I got some barley and flax bread rising. But I had beans on the brain. My food charts and maps wall showed Dapp, Stony Plain, and Bezanson (all northwest of Edmonton), and Bow Island (halfway to Medicine Hat), as locales where pulse growers resided. Exactly where did "local" end? In my cupboard, crammed behind the laird lentils, I found a package of white beans grown in Vulcan, 130 kilometres away.

The beans went into a pot of water on the stove, and I rummaged the freezer for ideas. If I was cooking, might as well do double duty: what to eat tomorrow? Katahdin lamb from growers near Olds was packed next to tubs of chicken stock and roasted tomatoes from Black Diamond. A few pieces of bison were jumbled with sausages, wild venison, and duck legs. Braised lamb shoulder with rosemary and onions? Cassoulet and confit? Barley risotto with grilled sausages? My brain ached. When confronted with too many choices, I tend to retreat, citing analysis paralysis. Maybe I should just think about lunch—how about a nice piece of cheese? Grilled Alberta Gouda on homemade bread? Simple. Much better.

Fed and watered, my brain back in gear, I settled on lamb for the next night's supper.

≈

By the middle of the afternoon, the beans were tender. I simmered the tomatoes with a few leeks into a melting fondue and dumped them into the bean pot, so good with braised lamb. Simplicity has virtue when you start with good ingredients. Every *baba* and *nonna* knows that.

My grandfather, an off-colony Hutterite farmer, had made wine from rhubarb and strawberries. In his honour, and because it was the middle of the afternoon on a grey winter day, I pulled the cork on a cherry wine made in Strathmore, an hour's drive away. Wine for me, wine for the marinade.

By then the bread dough was rising, and I pinched a handful for an impromptu pizza, reproducing the best I'd ever eaten, consumed one autumn evening beside the Canal du Midi in southern France. Topped with red-skin sliced potatoes and thyme, slathers of soft sautéed onion slivers, and smoky ham—or had it been bacon? sausage?—and a sprinkle of grated high-mountain cheese, gilded with heavy cream, it made a glorious transition to Canada.

Like my grandmother, I used duck fat: no olive trees for miles. I checked food scientist Shirley Corriher's book *Cook-Wise* to remind myself about fat profiles, and was relieved to learn (again—I wish I could remember this stuff!) that duck fat was 40 percent monounsaturated. That's the good fat, known to help reduce blood cholesterol levels. With duck fat, butter, and cold-pressed canola oil in my pantry, I could live without olive oil.

But, oh my, vegetables. In this long-sloping shoulder season's run-up to spring, I had no recourse but to the sturdy ones.

"Cauliflower is cabbage with a college education," Mark Twain once said. Poor man, he needed a better cook. The oven was fired up already for the pizza and bread, so I pulled apart a head of cauliflower, rolled the florets in melted duck fat and spread them on a baking sheet. In an hour, I'd have irresistible roasted cauliflower, mahogany and crisp. What did Mark Twain know?

The rest of the dough morphed into loaves. Their bottoms echoed dully as I hauled them from the oven later in the afternoon. The house overflowed with aromas. I settled on soup to go with the pizza, a satisfying use of those carrots from an endangered organic farm north of the city, its rich black soil surrounded by highway blacktop and desired by greedy town councillors for development. My grandmother would have recognized this meal. Some things don't change.

After supper that night, a little of the cherry wine went into some egg yolks to make a sabayon sweetened with honey. My son spooned the sabayon over cooked black currants and gooseberries, slid the plate briefly under the broiler, and offered me a dollop. Yum.

The lamb shoulder deconstructed itself into luscious layered flavours in the oven as the evening wound down, the day spent on food and cooking.

When I was a younger cook, still learning how the jigsaw of food fit, I tried to get every flavour I liked into one pot at the same time. As I've matured, I've absorbed the lesson that what grows together goes together. And to keep it simple, stupid. My braised lamb shoulder would devolve its leftover bits into shepherd's pie, just as the leftover currants and gooseberries were destined to morph into a streusel-topped crisp for breakfast. My frugal grandmother's lamp was still burning in my kitchen.

It was a rough few months transitioning into spring. My winter fare—influenced by our climate and geography—was plenteous in volume but limited in scope. It fed the prairie-born part of me but left my wannabe tropical giddy girl feeling denied and dissatisfied. My pragmatic nature emerged, shaking its head like a hungry bear looking for springtime tender nibbles. What to shrug at and buy, despite its origins? Only my inner bear knew what she really wanted. I quickly learned that I'd best listen, or there'd be hell to pay: denied a single bite of good dark chocolate, my inner bear-woman would rampage through the kitchen, sampling everything sweet, from jam to syrup to dried berries, and then settle on the chocolate, as well, at triple the calorie cost. Oy.

Vegetables were the weak link. April and May were balanced on the cusp of spring: the light had returned, the weather was gentle, but I wasn't fooled, nor was my stove. I wanted to garden, smell damp soil, feel dirt in my hands, then eat green young plants. But in Alberta, the soil was still chilly. All I had in my vegetable bin were spuds, beets, carrots, and those hard green Roundheads, cabbages, scraping down the sides of the barrel to the dregs of dining.

Cabbage is loaded with good things, but it gets boring when repeatedly cast as the star, like watching Hugh Grant play himself in movie after movie—Hugh as British PM, Hugh as naive bookstore owner, Hugh as philandering serial monogamist: cabbage with bacon, sausage, ham hocks, smoked pork, pancetta, bison bacon; cabbage with carrots; cabbage with dried berries and dried dillweed. I needed a trenchant dollop of Dame Judi Dench—as Queen Elizabeth I; as an Edwardian aristocrat; as M, James Bond's acerbic boss. So I ate turnips smashed with butter and honey; beans with bacon or ham hocks or both; sauerkraut and innumerable sausages. I loved them all, those plain but delicious and earthy dishes, but I craved what the prairie garden did not yet grow—the pungency of arugula, grassy asparagus stalks, gritty just-pulled carrots, a spring rabbit's diet.

All winter I debated the ethics of participating in a global economy. I surprised myself by—mostly—ignoring the vanilla bean paste on my shelves and occasionally eschewing my bear-woman's evening mouthful of dark chocolate. It was true that my purchase of Madagascar Bourbon vanilla beans and ethically raised chocolate gave employment and a market to Third World farmers, many of whom are women with little say in their farm's management. It was also true that abruptly ceasing to use tropical products—say, for instance, shutting down my caffeine habit—would leave those growers with only a local market, akin to carrying coals to Newcastle. But like my grandmother, I do buy coffee, chocolate, vanilla, and cocoa, luxuries worth the splurge. As a compromise, for my mid-afternoon tisane à la Hercule Poirot, I switched to drinking homegrown spearmint tisane instead of South African rooibos. Conversely, I didn't miss mangoes or papayas, but oh, I missed pineapple! Unfortunately, no pineapples materialized as gifts—the only way I allowed myself to enjoy the long-distance foods that I didn't judge as indispensable.

Despite the dearth of pineapples, gifts were generous and unexpected. Who was I to turn down presents from friends? Food gifts come from the soul, and declining them would have made me feel like a child throwing stones at her mother's greenhouse windows in mid-winter. So when a collection of my favourite Silk Road spices arrived from a Vancouver chef, I and my pots danced a curry-inspired *cumbia*. From an eastern friend, I received a square-necked bottle of Ontario maple syrup that I swigged from as if it contained hooch and I was a desperate drinker. My produce-importing buddy Roy gave me a bushel basket of Californian citrus that I hoarded like gold and amber as I converted its contents into marmalade, candied grapefruit rind, orange curd, Meyer lemon mousse, preserved lemon.

Late in March, another gift arrived in the post, Benedictine fruitcake laced with Kentucky bourbon from a friend on retreat at a monastery in Kentucky. The universe had heard me, and my friends unknowingly acted on my behalf.

Other foods materialized from closer to home. A spontaneous side-trip down a muddy gravel road sent me to a "duckery" one hundred miles away. This farm's duck prosciutto and duck "ham" were an unexpected pond of pleasure that I plunged into after a first, wide-eyed "Oh my God" luscious mouthful.

When I got home, grinning like a pirate returned from plunder, my son Dailyn just laughed. "Of course you stopped at a farm. Of course you brought home things to try. Of course." I sliced the prosciutto, slapped a slice into his hand, and watched his face change. "Oh. That's good. Can I have . . . ?" I sliced the rest. We shared. The duck farm had two more fans.

≈

In mid-April, I pulled my grandmother Sarah's 1921 *Five Roses* cookbook from my shelves. How had she gotten through her winters of discontent? Surely she'd felt some, living all her life on the prairie! Sarah's writing was snaky and faint, a tattoo along the outer skein of fragile paper, detailing wine-making, ketchup experiments, lemon squares, bread variations, countless pickles.

A phone call home filled in the blanks. "She canned two cases of every fruit in summer when it arrived from BC by truck," Mom recalled, "and saskatoons we picked on the farm. We had raisins, we had baking staples. But we never saw lettuce in winter!"

My mother, aunt, and grandmother had canned chicken and beef they'd raised themselves. Smoked sausages and hams had hung beside a side of beef in the smokehouse. Wheels of Ontario cheddar had foreshadowed the arrival of my southern Ontarian father. They'd eaten fresh oranges only at Christmas, but the Medalta crock of sauerkraut and the jars of pickles had lasted all winter. In the cold season, my mother could gather the odd egg "but only if the hens weren't suffering from chilly." My grandmother's baking, straightforward and uncomplicated, had never encompassed the mousses and mille feuilles I mastered at cooking school. She'd never had time for fancy, so she leaned on the simple things—bread, strudel, cookies, pie, squares. In her honour, I made apple and saskatoon cobbler for breakfast.

≈

Local means different things in different locales, a tiny slice of terroir. While in Tofino on the West Coast for my mid-winter birthday, I had joyously downed Dungeness crab, spot prawns, and Haida Gwaii halibut. Picking and eating perfect peaches the previous summer in Cawston, in the heart of the Similkameen Valley, I'd wept as the amber juice dripped down my face and arms. Calgary—where mid-winter fruit was non-existent and local fish limited to farmed tilapia, or trout fished from the Bow River—was similar to my grandparents' Saskatchewan farm, where I'd later live as a writer. In deep winter, I'm sure Gran longed for her garden: it had been a peaceful refuge for me as a child, and for my own sons when my mom tended it, my boys ducking through the tented pole beans, wandering among the sunflowers and corn, silk rustling like a queen's lace mantilla.

I didn't want to work as hard as my mother and my grand-mother had needed to. At that time, still in Calgary, I didn't live on a farm, or keep a cow, and I didn't till the soil behind a pair of draft horses. I didn't own a cream separator, although I remembered how to milk a cow, the slow heave of her flanks as I leaned my head on her side, her sweet grassy breath on my neck, the rhythm of the milk as it jazzed into the metal buck-et between my knees. As kids we had spooned heavy yellow cream from Mom's cranky cow onto our cereal, and splashed a bowlful of milk for the waiting cats.

I decided to ask Elna Edgar, the province's asparagus queen, for a few asparagus crowns. (The tangle of ferns that would engulf my Saskatchewan farmyard garden in a few summers after our move there were not yet a fact.) Asparagus was hope made tangible, spears spun from fragile ferns and sunshine after winter's absolutist mineral-fed root vegetables. A trip north to the asparagus patch, a day spent in the sandblasting wind. Elna gave me asparagus crowns as a gift. But putting the crowns in the ground was the easy part. Patience came harder.

My dwarf sour cherry trees—bred by University of Sas-katchewan professor Bob Bors in Saskatoon—were a good example of fruit growing for the short of patience. I'd planted them as twigs in 2003, when they'd first been released to the public, and they'd borne cherries within a year. Come sum-mer, they would again be heavy with fruit, ideal for tarts, cob-blers, jams.

Meanwhile, the rhubarb in the corner of the garden was aiming for world domination. I bought other hardy berry shrubs—saskatoons, strawberries, raspberries, black currants, and Siberian haskap, barrel-shaped purple honeyberries that had also been bred at the U of S—toward my goal of an entire-ly edible landscape.

But I didn't expect to grow all my produce. So I called Jonathan Wright. He and his partner, Andrea Thompson, had started a community supported agriculture (csa) farm near Beiseker, and named their endeavour Thompson Small Farm. Small was the new big, I thought admiringly as I drove out to visit and was the first to buy a share in the first season's crop. While I was there, I marvelled at Raven and Gwyneth, the Clydesdale draft horses, and the water buffalo that Jon and Andrea had acquired from the herd at Fairburn Farm, north of Victoria on Vancouver Island. The animals were their version of solar-powered, pulling in preference to tractors on their twenty-acre farm. "Animals tread more lightly on the soil," Jon told me. It was my first of what would be many investments in similar farms with similar hardworking farmers. I hoped, too, to learn how to harness and drive these enormous horses, in memory of my grandparents. Some things come full circle. When I got home, I started work on a poem about Jon and his mares.

≈

All that spring, as farmers do, I kept one eye on the sky and an ear to the crop reports, charting the rise in temperature along with skyrocketing prices for wheat and corn—the latter reportedly grown for biofuel, not food, which struck me as ludicrous.

I nearly cried when the first greenhouse-grown Albertan lettuces and tomatoes appeared at the market. What a relief! Those tomatoes were a pungent breath of renewal, and I carried home a bunch of living watercress like a bouquet, then wrote a poem to the last cabbage of the season.

My garden, east-tipped, south-facing, soaked up the warmth, and I placed my seeds sparingly, withstanding the temptation to sow them too thickly. Thinning is tedious, especially with carrots. Next were marigolds, leeks, candy cane and golden beets, and chard, then lettuces for heads and "cut 'n' come again" mixes.

This garden represented the first, and most immediate, of the concentric rings that marked my food's provenance. The peaches I loved, grown in the Similkameen Valley southwest of the Okanagan Valley, occupied the third ring. In between lay the lands of the living—local farms, including the CSA farm I subscribed to. I drove to the farm because I liked the chance to breathe in the smell of horses as Jon adjusted the harness of the Clydesdale mares, to imagine the leather reins in my hands, to see the land open beneath the metal blade.

Summer flowed from spring like a butterscotch sundae. My fridge bulged. One morning, crouching in a field west of Olds, I picked strawberries, eating them sun-warm as quickly as I could snap them free of the plant, just as I had as a child on Vancouver Island. At home, I made sorbet. Frozen scoops served with whole berries and a plateful of lemon thyme–infused cookies made the perfect summer dessert.

Winter's lack of greens was replaced by a rainbow of abundance—chard, spinach, arugula, mâche, beet tops veined with carnelian and amber. For lunch, I wilted handfuls of spinach in local butter, added a spoonful of southern Albertan chèvre, tossed it gently and ate it by the bowlful, loving the textural contrast of melting greens and smooth cheese. For supper, more vegetables—grilled bell peppers, grilled eggplant smeared with gouda, grilled carrots. I tossed carrots to Mojo, my miniature schnauzer, who loved them, too. Tootles to nearby growers gave my city-bred sons a chance to walk the fields. We drove east to an orchard near Strathmore, sat in the gazebo, watched the sunlit pickers, and bought a bottle of cherry wine for the boys' grandfather. A week later, we stood in wheat fields north of the city, talking shop with a farmer. I wanted some of his house-milled grains for my bread-baking habit, but had to wait for harvest. We left with full hands, though—eggs, vegetables—and the promise of pork as well as flour.

Every week, I visited a different farmers' market in the city, cherry picking the best produce. My counters, tabletop, and fridge were heaped to bursting. It was time for a neighbour-hood block party and feast. I debated spitting and roasting a whole lamb, but grilled a clutch of sausages and lamb chops instead. I spent an afternoon baking flatbread topped with every vegetable in the bin, and layering tomatoes and eggplant into an unruly approximation of moussaka. I tossed new pota-toes and beets in a gleaming jacket of cold-pressed canola oil with shards of minced basil and dillweed. Cucumber discs floated in a pool of homemade vinegar and sour cream. For dessert, I made my own mascarpone to accompany bowls of high-season berries. The cherries and sliced peaches had already drawn the eye of my six-year-old neighbour. Her moth-er, born in Moscow, divorced from an Algerian, had brought me her favourite Algerian dishes in the depths of my winter hunger, so that day I reciprocated with summery dishes.

≈

As the weather changed, we harvested the patch beside our deck, kneeling on the flat stones to pick robust mustard greens, carrots, the last of the herbs. Road trips added specialties from northeast of Edmonton, in the map's second ring—bottles of fruit wine from near Two Hills; smoky Ukrainian pork sausage from Vegreville, Vermilion, Viking. A double handful of wine vinegars gathered on an Okanagan winery trip—plus several cases of wine—added the necessary pucker of acidity to my prairie pantry. Any cook worth her salt and vinegar will cheerfully admit that those two condiments accentuate human happiness and cooking.

In mid-autumn, my friend Sarah-jane brought me a surfeit of tomatoes, and my sons came home for canning lessons. During the spring, they had observed the depleting stash of homemade condiments in my fridge. "We want to learn to can, Mom," they'd said, so I set up the blue enamel pot, the big stainless pans, the tongs, and the wide-mouth funnel, and I taught my boys how to put autumn away. We made chili sauce from a generations-old recipe passed down from my southern Ontarian grandmother, Doris, and piquant corn relish such as Sarah, my Hutterite maternal grandmother, always made. Pickles. Fruit in honey syrup. Jams. My sons were good cooks. They made a good team, trading jokes, potholders, and pans, and I was reminded, joyfully, of the reasons for never canning alone.

It was harvest, and I laid in supplies. In my freezer, I layered local duck legs, slabs of Berkshire pork, whole chickens, bison hump, lamb.

On the stove, basil and strawberries melded into a subtle pink jelly set with crab apples from the front yard. The black currants simmered into good manners, and came up smiling as alcohol-free honey-sweetened cassis puree, perfect for kir and cocktails.

"I guess I know what I'm giving as gifts this Christmas," Dailyn observed. He has made a habit ever since of giving handmade edibles. Food makes memories, and gifts of homemade food are diamonds in a climate of fast, mass-produced, and mediocre. With each bottle and jar, he gives a gift of the time he spent in the kitchen, a gift impossible to contain in tissue. Time has become the most precious commodity, and an investment in handmade is always tallied in time, love, and intentions.

Cases of peppers succumbed to the flames and were stacked in freezer tubs like paving stones for winter soups and cassoulets. We strung *ristras* of hot peppers from the pot rack to dry with bundles of cut herbs. Eggplant was stripped of its royal skin, roasted in fat slices, then consigned to garlic, oil, and spices. My sons watched avidly as a potful of duck thighs bubbled and simmered in their own fat, confit in the making. Jars accumulated.

Some foods stored themselves. My beets, carrots, and leeks lingered in the soil until I sent Dailyn out to free them. "Leek and potato soup, Mom," he announced, and scrubbed the two-tone lengths clean. That night's supper of soup, wilted greens, and poached eggs was the essence of simplicity, eaten on the deck by candlepower as the moon waned; it would become a standby a few years later when Dave and I would plant our raised beds on the farm.

It was a bellwether moment. My reconnection to a local diet came with unexpected benefits. A deeper sense of immediacy and place meant I ate what the moment and the weather rendered possible. And I remembered what has been forgotten in an era of globalized food commodification and pre-made meals: my family's food choices were slimmer if the fields and farms that fed us were tossed awry by rains, winds, drought, or cold.

Casting this net created a symbiotic network. I knew the people who grew my food, and they knew me. But the fact remains that for many Canadians, the time, money, and effort it takes to source local ingredients seems overly demanding. This indicts a society that does not recognize the primary importance of good food, and of cooking and eating together. The situation will not improve until consumers recognize that food is more than a commodity, and that locally grown will feed us better than what has travelled thousands of miles.

Now resident in Saskatchewan, with a new network of growers to supplement our garden, I am still pragmatic. In Canada, a year-round, 100-percent-local diet is neither balanced nor full on pleasurable, both prime considerations for a cook who loves what she does. But a mostly local diet from within my map's outer circle *is* possible, pleasurable, and meaningful. Pragmatism can include place, too.

I recently reread the meditations and aphorisms of the nineteenth-century French lawyer and gastronome Jean Anthelme Brillat-Savarin, as recorded in his 1825 tome, *The Physiology of Taste.* Quoting his friend and colleague Henrion de Pansey, he invoked place, as well, saying, "Tell me what you eat, and I shall tell you what you are."[1]

Let me tell you what I am. I am a fifth-generation prairie-dwelling Canadian. Here is my home. Here is where I live my life, seasoned with food that has travelled a brief distance. From farmgate to plate, the minerals within Canadian soil nourish my plants, then migrate through my blood and bones. When I travel far from home, the magnetized minerals in my body draw me home again, for another homegrown meal at my own table.

BELLOW
~ *after "Howl" by Allen Ginsberg*

On the occasion of the closure of Lakeside Packers,
Brooks, Alberta, September 2012.

I.

I saw the best heifers and steers destroyed by greed, hung to bleed and die after being dragged by chain through a system of dead ends, star-studded sky invisible to their staring eyes.

Cattle, fat but starving, bloated with fear, who cowered hock-deep in shit and urine, who bellered for their mothers, caught upon the mighty machinery of appetite, of avarice, of international trade and multinational commerce, of pork belly futures, of carcasses sold by live weight and transmuted into dead meat.

Cattle who had dreamed with shining eyes turned to the firmament of timothy fields and alfalfa in flower and brome grass and clover with its fading purple blossoms.

Cattle who were herded into drafty eighteen wheelers, feet failing them when the transport truck cornered too quickly on the highway to hell, who nightly prayed with the two-note call of their kind for deliverance, for saving, for return to field and water and grass and sky.

Cattle who smelled the black iron of bloodletting as they waited, whose nostrils flared wide and red as their sisters and brothers trampled their dignity into the mud.

Cattle who were lined up and stunned by the thousands each day, who fell to their knees as their eyes darkened, lives ending with a bolt or a bullet but no prayer.

Cattle whose blood drained and pooled, limbs gone spastic before blessed rigour arrived, who hung, hooks through hocks upon the chain, dripping their lives out.

Cattle whose skulls were ground into bone meal with femurs, scapulas, hooves.

Cattle whose eyes glassed into death by their millions each year, the buffalo slaughter of our generation, who cried out for intervention.

≈

II.

What politicians and capitalists colluded for your end? Bay Street! Where stockbrokers eat at trophy restaurants, who run with deaf ears and stopped-up eyes from clients asking for funds for school lunch programs. Parliament! Where the Minister of Finance's new shoes cost more than a food bank voucher's value and agriculture has devolved into agri-food commodities.

I'm with you in Lakeside, dark abattoir, E. coli slaughterhouse. In Lakeside, four thousand animals a day, two million a year, butcher building. Lakeside, 1,800 products recalled, meat cutting hovel. The chain, the glove, the bolt, the stun gun. I'm with you in Lakeside, on the killing floor.

WHALE
WATCHING

Aboard *Tenacious 3* in the Georgia Strait off Campbell River, Vancouver Island: I'm in my raincoat, hood up, facing the wind, alone on the deck. We've blown through several squalls already, which may be why Dave and a family of Hong Kong Chinese visitors are below decks with Captain Warren Schuhl and naturalist Mark Evans. They're all crowding the port windows, scanning the water's edge for bears and bald eagles—although we're really looking for whales.

When I see a dozen triangular black wedges scudding along the water's glittering surface a half mile away, a surge of adrenalin blossoms through my innards. Squinting through the smudges on my glasses, I recognize Pacific white-sided dolphins, looking exactly as Evans described them in a detailed on-board briefing about local marine wildlife. *Tenacious 3* is moving along at about twenty-five knots in rough chop, so I'm cautious while making my way down to the cabin, where I announce the sighting. The captain immediately swings the boat around to catch up with the skidding dolphins. All of us charge outside to hang over the railings, cameras in hand, and watch the dolphins ride our wake, rolling and leaping, diving and surfacing, obviously playing, for twenty minutes, before we speed up and resume course northward. They are notoriously difficult to photograph, fast-moving blurs of water and bi-coloured hides smearing together in my viewfinder's lens, and I finally give up on the effort and simply enjoy their presence through my own eyes. Letting the camera slip to rest is a relief akin to the relief I feel whenever I hide my cellphone: life carries on without a screen or lens to record it.

I'm on the West Coast with Dave on a writing assignment. But time is blurring like the dolphins through that camera lens: every moment on the coast reminds me of my childhood years spent on Vancouver Island, and of my early twenties, when I lived in Vancouver. The waterside is so verdant, so humid and rich with life, it feels a million years away from our life in dryland Saskatchewan. But as a kid, and later as a young woman, I took that lushness entirely for granted. The bounty extended to what we ate: wild salmon we caught ourselves, clams, mussels, oysters, crabs, halibut, tuna, snapper, cod, all the riches of a maritime life. In Saskatchewan, we go months without eating fish of any sort. It's all deathly expensive, a dwindling luxury writers on a budget can't regularly cop to—for ethical as well as financial reasons—despite urgings from the food police to eat fish regularly.

Earlier in the voyage we'd crossed Seymour Narrows, a five-kilometre stretch of Discovery Passage just north of Campbell River that connects Johnstone Strait and Georgia Strait, now called the Salish Sea. This is the route traversed by humpback and killer whales. Captain George Vancouver had explored around here in the late 1700s and had described Seymour Narrows as "one of the vilest stretches of water in the world."[1] He didn't know that the women of the region's Indigenous people—the We Wai Kai, Kwakwaka'wakw, and the Coast Salish Klahoose—had harvested the region's rich seafood offerings, especially in their clam gardens in the intertidal zones of the rocky coves that line the region.

Schuhl agrees with Vancouver's assessment. "That place is a boneyard," he says, nodding at Cape Mudge on the tip of Quadra Island, "the most dangerous waters around here."

Schuhl takes *Tenacious 3* around the thirty-foot whirlpool that whistles over the remains of Ripple Rock, once a twin-spired underwater mountain. It was blown up in 1958 in what was, at the time, the world's largest non-nuclear explosion. Its remains still roil the water, and I feel a landlubber's anxiety jostling my belly, Captain Vancouver's words echoing: a boneyard. Soil is my medium. Earth, and seeds, trees with roots, growing plants with half their being embedded in dirt, and the solidity and permanence that such things embody. On water, life feels uncertain. Impermanent. This channel, its whirlpools and vanished subterranean peaks, seems the essence of mutability, with death and a seafarer's watery grave hanging around its edges.

The irony is inescapable, given my current living situation, surrounded by water. At home in Saskatchewan, our house perches on a virtual island, the result of a flood in 2011 that created a lake of my land. Waterfowl, shorebirds, and water-loving animals live and feed just yards beyond my studio window. Each morning, I watch a pair of American avocets gangle at the shoreline, withstanding the territorial lunges and yakking of two American coots whose clumsy nest is precariously balanced on a bit of lumber wedged against the cattails. American. Imported since the flood. But biologists might say otherwise, that like the black snails I see along the water's edge, like the boreal chorus frogs who slept through winter in mud and emerged to serenade the waking world, that the call of my new little lake mimics the ancient glacial waterway that existed in another era. That all those creatures slept until the floodwaters arrived, and called, and woke them.

Their voices and doings feed my spirit, and my writing.

≈

It was because of the whales, and to witness a rare farmed-fishing success story—the annual Tofino spot prawn festival—that I had originally flown to Vancouver Island.

Spot prawns, native to North America's West Coast, have emerged as the posterchild of sustainable shellfish farming. In the past, most BC spot prawns were shipped live to Japan, leaving only the damaged and the dead for local consumers. But Vancouver chefs refused to believe that BC waters would produce such crap and created a spot prawn festival that revitalized demand, quality, and a flagging industry. BC spot prawns, all sustainably farmed, are now available flash-frozen across Canada, in a sensible extension of the sixty-day spot prawn season.

That afternoon in Tofino, at the festival on the dock, I peeled and ate platefuls of grilled spot prawns hot from the line of barbecues fronted by chefs in immaculate whites. Hundreds of people congregated around us. I was queuing up for a third helping when, in a spectacular display of nature at her finest, a pod of killer whales cruised into the harbour, their black and white markings stark against the blue sky as they breached, effortlessly upstaging the chefs and locavore activists. The whales were a large and vivid reminder of what was at risk, and of Gaia, the interconnectedness of all living things.

Tour boats are based where the whales are: on the west coast of Vancouver Island, in Tofino; up island, at Fort McNeil, where whale watching began in 1980; on the island's east coast in Campbell River; in Victoria; and on the continent's East Coast—a few years earlier, I'd visited Newfoundland with my youngest son, and we'd gone out from Trinity on a whale-watching boat (unsuccessfully) on the lookout for humpbacks. In Tofino, Charles McDiarmid, owner of the Wickaninnish Inn, pointed out whales in Barkley Sound to Dave and me, along with dozens of other diners in his restaurant. "Whale watching has helped Tofino emerge as a foodie destination," he said, deadpan, without glancing around at his busy white-tablecloth dining room.

But Evans, the naturalist, has a different view: "It's about connecting the public to the environment with minimal impact." He means minimal impact on the natural world. We have a globe's worth of proof of the negative impact humanity has wrought on the natural world. I know first-hand that nature's—and specifically, whales'—impact on humans can be positive and immense. My first sighting was during the March 2005 grey whale festival, when I spent half a day crouched in a low-in-the-water zodiac, entranced, tracking a pair of juvenile whales through Clayoquot Sound at their own level, not looking down at them from the deck of a tour boat. Flickering greenish light played off the whales' backs, eerie and magical. There was no explaining how I could feel connected to two behemoths so completely unconcerned with me, but I did.

≈

Soon after meeting the dolphins, we enter Nodales Channel and spend ten minutes watching a gawky young black bear on the beach of Sonora Island. Against a backdrop of towering Douglas fir, the bear turns up logs and rocks, looking for oysters and insect grubs. Hunger, I can understand, and I would remember the young bear hours later, when we'd sit down to a dinner of grilled salmon, and I would hope that she, too, had found a feast.

As we pass tiny Stuart Island, harbour seals and sea lions bark, their cries echoing down the narrow channel. Their voices remind me of my waterway at home, which hosts silent muskrats, elegant in their element as they cut through the water in a *V* to and from lodges heaped from bulrushes and cattails, but lumbering on land as they raid my garden for romaine hearts and corn stalks. I never hear their passing, these small creatures, the voiceless ones, but I feel pleasure when I see their bulbous heads, all that is visible as they cruise across the water, and I don't begrudge them their share of the garden. Their come-and-go daily presence, their lodges, their kits, all confirm the health of my unexpected flood-lake.

Four hours later, we emerge from the maze of passages where Schuhl steers through standing waves (a stationary wave caused by two equal currents meeting, often at a spot of sudden depth change), tidal currents, and whirlpools. By now I have seen so many bald eagles that it seems almost commonplace to spot yet another as we pass a green shed that Evans, the naturalist, identifies as one of many salmon farms that dot the coast. The harshness of its rough building—surrounded by shadows that understand the richness of rain and soil, Douglas fir and cedars climbing to the clear-cut strip above—emphasizes the intrusion of what it houses. Farmed Atlantic salmon are being raised in an ecosystem where wild Pacific sockeye, chum, spring, chinook, coho, and pink salmon have fed whales and bears and seals and dolphins, and Indigenous Peoples, for eons. Nets, weirs, gaffs—the tools used varied, as did the storage and preservation of the catch—smoking, sun-drying, the roe toasted but sometimes fermented, and always by the women. The silver fish were revered and honoured, and the Indigenous Pacific Coast cultures considered salmon immortal.

≈

Immortality might have helped. Sadly, commercial overfishing has disproved this cultural belief. Salmon has been off my plate for a long time, bedeviled by the conundrum facing diners worldwide: Do I contribute to the death of an overfished species by eating wild-caught Pacific salmon? Or do I contribute to ecological pollution and potential territorial takeover by eating farmed Atlantic salmon? In 2010, for the first time in a dozen years, I allowed myself to purchase and cook wild Pacific salmon. That year, thirty million silver fish had made the run up the Fraser River, unprecedented numbers that cast hope on a fishery that faced dying like the East Coast cod fishery.

I'm not alone in my bedevilment: eating fish at all has become a luxury, with overfishing the biggest and most easily solved issue, says an expert, Mike McDermid, who at the time managed the Vancouver Aquarium's Ocean Wise program. He believes that limiting or banning wild fishery is not the ultimate solution. "We know we cannot support the demand for seafood without aquaculture," he says a few weeks later by phone. "We need to figure out how to sustainably farm fish."

Fishermen as farmers is not new: this ancient practice— simple, symbiotic, low intensity, low impact—originated when carp or tilapia swam in flooded Asian rice fields. Fish and rice were harvested as part of a local diet that encouraged diversity, environmental symbiosis, monetary stability, and overall health.

One-third of the world's fish is farmed, but there are drawbacks if it is approached as a feedlot, just as with cattle. Dr. George Leonard of Ocean Conservancy, speaking in June 2010 on the CBC radio show *Quirks and Quarks*, said, "The feed required by piscivores (fish-eaters) like salmon is the Achilles heel of the aquaculture system."[2] Salmon, at the top of the food chain, require copious amounts of fish meal, fish oil, and smaller fish. That means farming fish to feed the fish, which is costly and requires transportation thus unsustainable. All Atlantic salmon sold in Canada is farmed. Perhaps it's time to rethink what we take from the drink. Why raise and eat carnivores? Why not farm herbivores like tilapia, catfish, and carp?

In 2010, McDermid estimated that over one hundred Canadian inland and ocean farms sustainably produced tilapia, trout, char, halibut, and a variety of shellfish. What they eat is a hot button: some farmers convert their herbivores into piscivores by giving them fish meal for faster growth. Does this make them a worse ecological choice than fish from farther away that were raised on a sustainable vegetable-based diet? It's the same question we routinely ask ourselves about locally raised beef, chicken, and lamb versus meats from "away."

Fish farms fall into two categories: inland and open water pens. Generally speaking, inland farms do a better job of controlling problems than open water pens, although black tiger prawns raised in Southeast Asian ponds are a glaring negative example. In open water pens, population density leads to increased parasites, which can then also infect wild fish stocks; large amounts of excrement are generated into the ocean; inmate escape is a risk; and landscape and seascapes are adversely altered, including the formation of algae bloom that reduces the oceans' oxygen supply. Off-shore pens need to be robust to withstand rough seas, and costs of transporting finished fish are high—in dollars and in carbon-based fuel.

≈

"We don't guarantee anything. This is not the zoo," *Tenacious 3*'s co-owner, Geord Dunstan, says when we dock beside the ferry terminal in Campbell River. "These are wild animals in their own habitat, although we do all in our power to find whales."

Although we travelled fifty miles today without seeing orcas or humpback whales, I'm not disappointed, but still flooded with the exhilaration that coursed through me as we watched the dolphins leap and curvet. It's a common response, Dunstan says. "Usually there are so many other wildlife sightings going on [during a cruise] that people are happy. A lot of our guests are not familiar with the BC coast. Being in that natural wild environment is enough to elicit a response of awe—increasingly, urban people are not connected with nature."

I know that's true, but it stuns me all the same. Nature is part of my quotidian, anxiously so sometimes, as chafing frets about ticks during the summertime, but more frequently as pleasure—the surge of shared belonging whenever I watch the wildlife I live beside, the sense of satisfaction when I recognize another species of waterfowl or shorebird on my morning walks. A large part of my enjoyment is the auditory experience of life beside a lake: the thrumming of frogs; the lilting melody of chickadees and meadowlarks; the hummingbirds' whirring wings as they hover at the feeder; the cantankerous squawking of the coots; the geese honking as they arrive and leave like metronomes each spring and fall; coyotes carolling each evening. I want everyone I know to have those sounds as their daily backdrop to life, and can't imagine giving them up, but must eventually, when the lake recedes and dries up. I sense myself as part of the Gaia web, the symbiotic connection of life force on the planet. It's a too complex and too perfectly devised world to be otherwise, although when I am confronted with removing ticks on my dog's coat, I wonder about the role of such insects.

Near Campbell River's waterways, about three hundred northern "resident" orcas (which eat salmon, not small mammals) live in highly structured family groups. Marine biologists track, photograph, and count them annually. "They are incredible, complex animals. To see them isolated and alone in aquariums is heartbreaking," Dunstan's business partner, Heike Weiske, says wistfully. "A lot of junk goes into our oceans and ends up here from as far away as Japan. If seeing free whales strikes a chord, people can maybe make changes in their everyday lives to benefit the environment as a whole."

≈

A week later, I'm on the flying bridge of *Wasco* ("sea wolf" in Haida). We leave the calm water of Clayoquot Sound behind for open water, and spray drenches my face as the boat smashes through five-foot swells. I'm queasily wondering why I'm here when I overhear the Englishwoman sitting behind me tell her husband, "This is a mistake!"

It's a relief when we pull into a quiet inlet off Flores Island. The pilot cuts the power. As the boat drifts, he points out a pair of logs rolling close to shore. "A grey whale and her calf," he says. We wait for a tail or flipper, but cascading plumes of spray are our only clue as the whales surface and blow. A dozen boats bob by and the Englishwoman asks if we can get any closer. "No," the pilot replies. Later, he explains that marine life guidelines set by Fisheries and Oceans Canada forbid contact within one hundred metres.

The trip back to harbour is mild. We gaze at bald eagles, seals, and otters as we pass through Clayoquot Sound, adjacent to Meares Island, which was fiercely protected from clear-cutting in the 1980s and the 1990s by local environmentalists. Eco-tourism has replaced logging and fishing as the new West Coast boom, and whales are the big ticket—migrating grey whales on Vancouver Island's west coast, and orca, humpback, or minke whales in the Salish Sea. The whales aren't always hard to spot, but even when they are hidden, Pacific white-sided dolphins, seabird rookeries, seals and sea lions, bald eagles on the wing, and bears are common.

Years later, I still eat salmon only rarely, still stumbling over our heavy-footed stance on our planet, still searching for what cannot be easily seen. But convinced in part by the wildlife I live beside, I have accepted that even if I don't see a whale or snap the ultimate whale-watcher's photo on the water, the experience of proximity to wildlife is awe-inspiring and necessary to our humanity. Magic exists, in unexpected prairie lakes as surely as in the oceans.

SLOW DOWN,
DAMMIT

I am lying in my bathtub drinking tea and thinking about a comment a friend made when he wandered into a local coffee shop where I sat: "I feel guilty if I sit down and drink coffee and read the paper." He was perfectly serious, and didn't join me, but got his latté to go, and off he went, to his appointment, to work. I stayed where I was, drinking coffee and reading the paper. No guilt then, and none now as I luxuriate in my bath.

It's the middle of the day. I do have deadlines. But I am not working. I am not pretending to work. I am simply in my tub, drinking tea.

You may think that taking a bath in the middle of a workday is totally self-indulgent. But rest is not self-indulgence, nor one of the deadly sins. It doesn't even rate as a misdemeanour; it's a necessity.

Many of us do not allow ourselves the time to sit down with a newspaper and cup of coffee or tea, never mind a good book or a bath break. Instead, we have made a virtue of busy-ness, of to-do lists, and whip ourselves into a frenzy of deadlines, with an ungenerous serving of guilt for ourselves and for the others in our lives. No leisure time is allowed. We have created a rat race, but what are we racing toward? Or, perhaps closer to the truth, what are we racing from? And who wants to be a rat anyway?

A smart woman restaurateur once told me, "Creativity is the act of a rested mind." It didn't register then: I was twenty-seven. But now, with more than a few years gone by, I sometimes remember that she is right, and I head for my bathtub.

It is not just about resting our minds. We need to rest our bodies—what the poet Mary Oliver calls "these soft animals." The fragile frames we inhabit and often ignore are a vital part of the human package of awareness and creativity. As with our cellphones, we need to recharge our batteries. And, as the woman at the garden centre said to me when I explained I didn't want to turn off my car because it needed a new battery: "Honey, we all need new batteries." Sometimes, we need that, too.

The things that recharge me may look like surprisingly small things: baths, a good meal, a walk, fresh-cut flowers in the house, time with a good book, a hug, and, surprisingly, exercise. As it does for the Japanese novelist Haruki Murakami—who has run over two dozen marathons!—a long run clears my mind, reinvigorates my body, and yes, restores my soul.

I have come to believe that our lives are defined by those small things, the pearls that, strung together, comprise the necklace of our lives; no small irony lies in the truth of pearls originating as irritants to oysters just as the small things that ultimately define us are sometimes initially perceived as irritants.

Our lives are recipes, and we are the bakers. When my grandmother taught me to make apple strudel, the unspoken message was the importance of observing—and trusting—what my senses told me. But not from a distance. She and I got our noses close to the bowl of yeast, to smell its bubble and hear its hiss—was the time come to start mixing the dough? Later, I needed to touch the half-baked strudel to assess how raw or done it was, something only my fingers and eyes could gauge, and only close-up. The small details are there for us to notice, and are the signs of the natural world, the elementals. As William Blake wrote in 1799 in a letter to the Reverend John Trusler: "To the eyes of the man of imagination, / Nature is Imagination itself. / As a man is, so he sees."[1]

Seeing the world up close is a slow event that lasts a life-time, and the view is better from the valley floor than from the four-lane highway. During the past years, I drove through western Canada from Winnipeg to Whitehorse. Lucky for me, I found the off-switch, turned off my cruise control, and drove at a slower pace instead of blindly speeding through one anon-ymous town after another.

I learned to stop, too. Life is more than somewhere en route to elsewhere. It's the picnics, the detours down dusty side roads that create memories—a life. One year, driving through northern Alberta, I stopped beside the Peace River and ate ice cream beneath that great escarpment, and then I rode a ferry across the river at dawn, saluting the sun as it forded with me. Another year, my boot nudged ice crystals that shimmered like silver asparagus on the banks of the Yukon River in downtown Whitehorse, briefly blooming in May, melted in June. Farther north, in Dawson, sleepy town of writers, past Lake Lebarge, I witnessed the currents of the Yukon and Klondike Rivers flowing side by side, two rivers within one pair of banks. And another year, from the rear vestibule of a train, lonesome whis-tles dragging in the sky behind us, along the twisting turns of the Kicking Horse River, I saw up close the red-bellied salmon leaping in the autumn river bed.

From every river—the Yukon, the Whitehorse, the Red, the mighty Peace—I carried home small pieces of stone and piled them around my house, reminders of the earth's slower clock. But you don't need rocks on your bedside table to change pace. Tangibles beyond river and rock lie closer to home. Sometimes I spend a day in bed, with a book or my lover, or a pup, or alone. I don't answer the phone. Don't turn on the computer. And I do it guilt-free. The trick is to choose something that is at once inside and outside yourself. Try painting, or writing verses, or getting a kitten, or helping out at the homeless shelter. Give your change to the squeegee girl who washes your car's windows. Cook with a child—now there's a slow process, with results as unpredictable as life.

Consciousness governs the clock. When I slow down my external existence and pay attention, the spin within my body slows down, too, permeated with the small things: tea in the tub; blood in my veins; rivers in their banks; stars in the sky. Their flow is inexorable, and all we can do is surrender. We are fools and egotists to think that our actions matter greatly within the great clock in the sky, the wheel of the sun, and the wide arcing swing of the solar system.

One of my favourite photos is of my oldest son and me, taken by his father when our son was just three years old as he and I sat beside the Bow River on Prince's Island. It was sunset. The river flowed by. My sons are twenty-nine and thirty-four this year. Time is the ultimate river.

Although we are all born human, we must choose to be humane. Humanity resides in the small choices. Our actions reveal our selves. We are not rats. Reset your clock. Resign from the race and reside within the human one. The poet Charles Reznikoff wrote:

After I had worked all day at what I earn my living,
I was tired. Now my own work has lost another day,
I thought, but began slowly,
and slowly my strength came back to me.
Surely, the tide comes in twice a day.[2]

LOVE AFFAIR
WITH A WOLF

A Wolf owned my soul when I was younger. Sleek as an athlete, black as a well-seasoned cast-iron pan, inclined to fiery outbursts, he seduced me. He turned me into an oven junkie for life, side effect of an affair that dates back more than twenty-five years to when I acquired a restaurant with my former husband, Don.

At the time, I was a young mother and a chef, ambitious, obsessed: nothing but owning *my own* restaurant would do. We remortgaged our house, cashed in our savings, borrowed from Don's parents, then ran our business on a skin-tight budget, a business style I'd never endorse for anyone. Our pockets were not deep, the place was not big, and we were novices—despite my cooking school training and restaurant experience, despite Don's accounting acumen.

The joint had been a coffee shop, funky and wide-windowed, complete with coffee roaster, long oak bar, and spinning chrome stools. Our landlord was a collector of tchotchkes and antiques: a pair of calliope ponies pranced the wooden railings between the two levels, and ceramic dolls graced an upper ledge. The chairs were mismatched pressed-backs, antiques that didn't quite live up to the abuse they faced daily, and the tables were small hardwood squares worthy of a French bistro. We moved the roaster upstairs to a room behind our common office, and made the main floor into a functional restaurant by adding a Wolf range to the open kitchen that could barely accommodate one cook at the line.

This Wolf wasn't a *Canis lupus*. He was a twenty-three-inch beauty of a stove, a compact, gleaming commercial range, the heart of my restaurant. Hot, he was—can you say hot? The day the gasfitter charged the line and came upstairs to tell me the stove was ready to fire up, I left a meeting with my favourite sales rep and hurried downstairs, sales rep, gasfitter, and my husband on my heels.

The stove sat in its stainless steel alcove, gleaming, latent: four red knobs for the burners, one for the oven; inside, three metal racks. I wanted to do something solemn and ceremonial to mark what I knew was a sacred moment, but what came out was unrehearsed and childish. I whooped, I danced, the charge of a thousand volts of sunlight coursing through my blood, more potent than any sexual adventure or drug. Then I calmed, and struck a match, imagining the whispering smoke of a sage smudge. Four burners swooshed into being. I lit the oven, said a wordless blessing, and gently closed the door. I was ready. The salesman, his jaw dropping, traipsed upstairs with me after I extinguished the flames. "You go, girl," he said, and meant it.

~

We blew our budget on the Wolf, $2,500 used, a lot of money back then, and we couldn't afford the exorbitant stainless steel hood fan and air circulation unit that ensured ventilation while sautéing. It meant I couldn't fry foods. So I learned to love my oven.

All ovens are different. Like dogs, they may look sort of the same, but their temperaments are as different as schnauzers and salukis. But every oven has a hot spot. It took me a few weeks to find it in my Wolf. The gasfitter came back and verified the accuracy of the oven's internal temperature gauge, because ovens' external dials do not always register a true temperature. A variance as slight as twenty-five degrees Fahrenheit can mean the difference between a bread loaf that drops like the Grand Canyon or one that rises like Alberta's rolling foothills.

There is much more to the oven than turning out the perfect pie, or cookies for the in-laws: in an oven, a cook can brown more than bread or meat. A cook with oven-faith can roast, and braise, and brown, and caramelize fruit; can crisply cook bacon or pancetta, can oven-roast rosemary-kissed wedges of spuds, yummier than french fries. Even better are simmered potatoes with lemon and stock and garlic. A panful of those Greek-style spuds has crispy bits enclosing melting centres that put the best chocolates to shame.

≈

The stove I have the earliest memories of was wood fuelled, in some ways a mirror of my grandmother, flour-dusted and inviting, with rounded-off edges, the kind of stove a girl would pull a stool beside to lean on the warm enamel while the cookies baked. The reservoir was full of warm water, tempting enough to persuade the splash into a basin on a cold morning. Wood went to the flames through concentric rings that opened from the top of the firebox. The oven was underscored by a warming oven, where I hid socks and sweaters, toasting them for quick dressing on winter mornings.

With Gran, with that wood stove, I learned to make cookies, which are not as simple as people imagine. Those little discs of sweet dough follow the truism that the simplest things require the best ingredients: simplicity is a magnifying glass that enhances all that is good and not-so-good. It is also true that the simplest things illustrate principles most succinctly. I knew none of that, didn't realize that cookies could be any more complicated than watching my grandmother light the fire, mix up cookie dough, bake the rounds, and share the splendid results. That was how it worked. I didn't know that bakers are born, not made. I thought anyone could bake, that a wood stove was an obliging beast, easily managed. I had yet to learn that types of firewood and their water content have as much to do with a cookie's success as the sugar that defines a cookie's nature. That sugar is bipolar, contributing both tenderness and crispness. What I knew was contained in that kitchen, illuminated by love and my grandmother's matter-of-fact generosity: make the cookies, bake the cookies, share the cookies.

≈

Years later, newly married, the first stove I had grown-up relations with was far too old for the quick and eager cook I had grown into. A neophyte to adult life and needs, I left the old electric coil in charge of a glass double-boiler of cinnamon rice while I went upstairs and tended my first baby. When disaster struck, thoughtlessly, carelessly, then remorselessly, and the double-boiler boiled dry, I mopped the dead rice from the burner and consigned the broken glass to the great sand mill in the sky. That old stove had seen more than its share of baby food, and it wanted, like the anxious young mother who had mistakenly left it to its own devices, to lie down and rest its weary bones.

After that came a cold-hearted stove that resented its role, begrudging the lifeblood that is a stove's best attribute. The kitchen that housed it was cold, too; the room and the stove presented a united front. Visitors unconsciously retreated to the den, where a real fire crackled a welcome. Within a few months of our arrival, my husband and I removed the three of us to a more embracing home.

The next stove was old, as well, but imbued with the character and fierce pride of the widow who had shared its life. Like her, it was tiny, a veritable shoebox, and one of its three gas burners had winked and gone out one last time. Its miniscule oven taught me good manners and the thoughtful art of boning turkeys before stuffing them—refilled and reshaped but far less imposing without the skeleton—into its wee cave for roasting. When we bought its upscale replacement, that old gas stove sat for patient years in our garage, awaiting a reincarnation that never came, covered in dust, cobwebs, and indignity, pride extinguished and gas line severed like an artery.

In my current life, I share my kitchen with a gas stove cursed with a flaky computer panel, and I often find myself wishing for a stove without anything computerized. We spent thousands of dollars on our arrival at the farm in 2010 to run a natural gas line into our yard—a half-kilometre from the road—and this stove serves us well enough: I bake, fry, braise, roast. We eat. Our meals are not at a distance from our daily life—they are the start, and the heart. We eat, we write, walk, work, play. We eat again. Amen.

≈

In 1992, committed to my own joint in a new but cramped restaurant space, I mooned for months over the Wolf as it languished in a restaurant supply shop while my contractor built shelves and brought in walk-in refrigerators. To make room, he moved walls, shelving, and cupboards in the tiny open kitchen, creating a steel-lined alcove, a symbolic den of metal. Then I loosed the beast. Together, my Wolf and I braised succulent lamb scented with curry; studded pork loin with rosemary and prunes; smoked eggplant in a blackened wok; coaxed apples and pastry into butterscotch-glazed tarte Tatin unions; baked garlicky focaccia and crusty ciabatta; grilled asparagus; roasted tomatoes, flank steaks, vegetables; gilded almonds; whisked up lemon curd and passionfruit-scented peach mousse; simmered quinoa and lentils and flageolets.

Beyond the counter, small oak tables crowded with my restaurant's clients filled and emptied, filled and emptied. Customers came, ate, came back. Reviewers made their comments, and my kids went from hanging out with me in the basement prep kitchen to leaving me notes on my pillow at home, asking when I'd come home. Two years later, my failing health sent up smoke signals.

In the cold ashes of burnout, I sold everything, including the Wolf. I've mourned my infidelity ever since. The beast was well-mannered but uncertain; why was I handing the leash to new, untried cooks who knew nothing of it? As I walked away to my waiting sons and husband, I wept. Three months later, I tiptoed back in through the front door, sat at the counter, peered across its oaken barrier to where the Wolf sulked, its pilot lights clogged, its flames paled to yellow from hot blue. The new owners' menu listed canned soups, baked eggs, soggy quiche, white-bread sandwiches. I wept again, left without ordering, didn't return.

I lost touch with him. Rumours surfaced that he passed from hand to hand. Me, I cried for years, looking over my shoulder at the love I'd left behind when I'd walked out of my restaurant.

But I have not adopted caution. I still loose my latest stove, and sometimes let it run full throttle. The feeling has changed, though: I no longer expect to feel that intensity, the intense passion of the wild and brilliantly lit fling I shared with a Wolf. I will never own another restaurant, but in another life or in a dream, I may own an Aga, the British cast-iron cube stove. The one with all the ovens. Four ovens for an oven junkie . . . heaven.

SHELL GAMES

I was seven when we arrived on Vancouver Island from northern Alberta's slanted summer light. My brothers and sister and I were used to packing up and moving every year or two from air force base to base. We'd lived in a string of unremarkable houses, from Chicoutimi to Cold Lake to Winnipeg to overseas, the latter in buildings I have no recollection of. This time, Mom and Dad parked the trailer and pitched a tent on the beach. Kin Beach, outside Comox, became our home while we awaited the construction of our new house.

For us kids, it was paradise. The tent was snugged in a quiet little dell, fronted by a stand of Douglas firs, a cove of quiet behind the high tide driftwood and the blanket of kelp that surged onto the sand dunes and collected in heaps against the logs. Digging through the damp seaweed, avoiding washed-up starfish and sand dollars and scuttling tiny crabs, extricating a piece of bull kelp—all were acts of bravery for new coastal dwellers. We adapted quickly. Chasing my sister and brothers, hopping from log to log, snapping the kelp like a whip, was pure pleasure.

Above us, on the escarpment at nearby Point Holmes, Voodoo jets screamed into the air force base, but we were too busy with shell games to notice. At low tide, we swarmed across the slick rocks and stones, filling our buckets with oysters, wet and ridged layers of calcified time, moon-glow alabaster shells. The buckets wobbled beneath outstretched arms as we leaped from log to log, back to the beach fire that waited for us. Pitching the oysters in a heap, back to the beach for clams, shovels in hand, waiting for the betraying squirts of water that showed the hidden treasure.

Digging clams was a mug's game. No sooner would we put shovel to sand and flail down a few inches, we'd spot another squirt a few feet away, and in looking away, lose track of the current prize. Run to the new squirt, dig down quickly to locate the clam. When the bucket was finally full of sand-jacketed clams, we sluiced them with seawater and draped handfuls of damp seaweed on top. For sound effects, we stomped the fattest rackweed we could find.

≈

My mother was smart, and frugal, with five kids to feed on a corporal's pay. She taught us to forage, although at the time I didn't know that was what we were doing. I did know we had little money: later that fall, on a drenching-down rainy day, we would move from the beach onto the treed yard after the foundations for our house had been poured. Our house was a scavenger's make-do project, built partly from lumber milled from our own trees at a nearby mill, and partly from reclaimed lumber from the walls of a schoolhouse scheduled for demolition, as were the massive windows, the fir flooring, even the square-edged nails we pulled and painstakingly straightened. I didn't realize until I was an adult that what was happening was foraging, repurposing, recycling. In this era, my folks would be considered cool and hip, *uber*-environmentalists, but back then, everything looked old or chintzy, and felt grimy somehow, with previous use. Shameful. I felt it acutely, and knew it was because we were poor.

We had homemade toys. My doll house was carefully constructed, two storeys, painted, decorated, but homemade, of cardboard. My weekly allowance would never hold a candle to what my classmates—whose dads were sawmill workers, fishermen, pulp-and-paper workers, miners, and lumberjacks, every bit as blue-collar as ours—spent with fanfare on penny candy. Despite the lack of what we considered a suitable allowance, we ate well, and never went hungry. The rare walk down the hill and past the high school to the corner store to buy candy was one I often undertook alone. It was still a safe world.

We foraged for food, too: on every trip to the beach, we brought home things to eat—wild salmon occasionally, grunion by the bucketful when they were running and beached themselves in silvery strands on the beach, mussels, and clams most often, for bacon-scented clam chowder. And for clams stuffed with peppers and onions, bread crumbs on top, crisped under the broiler.

We picked oysters, too. I met the most famous bivalve that summer we lived on the beach.

≈

Life on Vancouver Island was defined by weather, most of it wet. That summer on the beach, it rained. Poured. Sprinkled. Misted. Dumped. All water. We got used to it. "You won't shrink!" Mom said, hustling us outside the tiny camper trailer or tent in our raincoats. But when cousins arrived from Ontario, they were dismayed by the wet. Non-stop rain collecting in the boat while we fished for salmon. Rain seeping through the tent roof, rain puddling in the trenches we dug to tunnel away the water. Damp sleeping bags, dogs that smelled doggy, and rain-shy clams that became more coy than usual. The driftwood logs were slicker than ever as we hopped our pursuit games down the beach, but the oysters looked otherworldly in the dull light. They gleamed, flat alabaster, their shells as ornate as dancehall girls' ruffles and swirls, calcified into dense jackets almost impossible to penetrate with a shucking knife.

We picked oysters by the dozens. Then we hunkered down, jackets and oysters steaming by the fire, and showed our visiting cousins how to eat like seasoned islanders. We ate oysters by the hundreds. Drizzled with lemon. Dashed with Tabasco. Scalloped and fried and dolloped with tartar sauce. For stew, Mom hoisted the big pot, buried its blackened base in the embers, threw in handfuls of onion and chunks of butter, hissing as the rain spit down. Bay leaves, a wisp of thyme, a jug of milk, then she ladled in dozens of raw oysters she'd patiently shucked while the rest of us had done kid things. The oysters emerged milky and fat, gleaming with butter and bits of onion, scooped into deep bowls.

"Quick!" Mom said. "Crack in the crackers and eat it before the crackers get soggy." But the crackers always sank to the bottom of the bowl.

It rained oysters that summer. We ate stew by the gallon, briny-sweet and cloying, scented by the sea and the sea breeze as it blew in off the beach. Every night, we steamed oysters open on the fire, our heaps of discarded shells attracting the scavenger gulls like an ancient midden. Finally, I couldn't countenance another oyster. No stew. Not one more raw or steamed or broiled or baked. Couldn't abide the smooth texture, the slick feel as it went from hand to mouth, from living to lunch. I was seven. I gave up oysters for good.

≈

So I thought. I became a chef, eventually cooking and working inland, in Calgary. I became a vegetarian, too, had given up meat before I arrived in a carnivore's community, and only returned to an omnivore's diet that included fish when I was carrying my second child.

In 2008, I found myself back on the West Coast, writing about shellfish, on an oyster beach along the coast of Cortes Island, just off Desolation Sound. On the ferry across from Quadra Island, I had stared at the map, a squiggling hieroglyphic of sounds and inlets and ocean depths, then sketched it in my journal. X marked the spot where I was to find Brent Petkau, an oysterman, waiting for me on his beach.

Brent was a man on a mission, to not only convert "his" people into oyster consumers, but to raise the profile of this bivalve beloved of lovers, an aphrodisiac sought by many over the millennia. His motive was as much environmental as carnal. Oysters filter sea water. That makes them important barometers of human waste management and water management. So when I met Brent, he was armed only with his oyster knife and his love of oysters. We went out in his boat and I watched him pull up his lines. It was easy to think of him as a farmer as I watched him kneel in his waterproof bib overalls and gumboots on the stony intertidal beach of his oyster lease. As generations of Indigenous coastal women had done before him, Brent had built a clam garden, manually moving rocks and stones to form breakwaters and shelters for clams and oysters. The beach was littered with heavy sacks awaiting shipment to restaurants across Canada.

Netted sacks of empty oyster shells lay leaching in the sun. Brent would take them to Pendrell Sound in August, when the warm water runs white with oyster spawn. The shells would be tucked into opened twists of two-ply twine, to dangle in thirty-foot lengths from rafts. On each shell, one hundred tiny dots would accumulate, each dot a spawn seeking a chance to grow into a tiny spat, which he would transplant to another stretch of beach along his lease. Becoming a full-size oyster takes from two to five years.

Brent dumped the oysters on the beach, calling them Royal Cortesans, a deliberate double entendre, a tip of the hat to Cortes Island as well as to their Japanese origins. I recognized them as glistening Royal Miyagi oysters, the ruffled, deeply fluted and layered Pacific beach oysters of my childhood. I'd learned in the intervening years that the species *Crassostrea gigas*, the Pacific oyster, had arrived on the West Coast from Japan—where they have been farmed for centuries in Miyagi Prefecture, northeast of Tokyo on the island of Honshu—perhaps barnacled to ocean vessels' hulls, in the early 1900s.

"Want one?" he asked. I shook my head, but he persisted. A misstep. "Human beings are not squeamish about oysters the way they can be about other animals they eat," he said, "because oysters don't bleed, and they don't have eyes to look back at you."

I must have registered my dismay, because he backed off. "This is the ideal place to eat oysters," he said mildly, sitting back on his heels, waving at the pristine beach, the logs.

As I studied the scene, I was wrenched back into my childhood, that idyllic summer on Kin Beach. What looked like a still life on first inspection was teeming with activity and life. Slow-moving whelks, propelling themselves a centimetre at a time, carved intricate furrows in the sand, leaving curving hieroglyphics as they crossed the slow-moving current to the sea. A tiny crab rolled one whelk over and over in the shallow water, grappling with the smooth coiled shell. A heron stood one-legged among the rocks, and a trio of harbour seals sunned themselves in the wan light. Cobalt-black mussels imitated rackweed, clinging to rocks, motionless in the tide. A dead jellyfish was a flamboyant puddle of pink staining the sand. Tiny geysers erupted, revealing the hidden beds of clams beneath the surface. Two bald eagles were motionless on a huge rock on the water's edge. A long ways off, wolves prowled the shore, hungry for seals.

The scene reassured me, and I finally nodded. A flick with Brent's shucking blade, then he reached upward from where he sat and held out an oyster. It was open, its grey flesh hiding most of the mother of pearl shell. I took the shell, held it to my lips. I could see a fragment of shell, imagined its shale-like texture on my lips, then the slick muscle of the oyster, and quailed. It was too big to swallow whole.

"Take a bite. Don't just swallow it. Chew," he urged.

My teeth sank into the meat. Holding my food in my hands, mere footsteps away from where it had been harvested, I'd never felt so primal—even as a carnivore in Calgary, where I'd learned to eat steak and lamb and pork with gusto. The oyster between my teeth was toothsome, tender, succulent, sweet. And briny. Somehow, that oyster tasted better than the hundreds I'd remembered—more like the sea. The lingering memory of slickness, of cloying, of gagging sweetness, disappeared for good, shucked and discarded as cleanly as Brent's shells on the beach at my feet. I ate the first one and held out my hand for another.

Later that evening, several other fishermen and women joined us for a meal of shrimp and, yes, oysters. We chatted about the weather, like any other farmers gathering for a meal, but the difference was one of degree—if a fisherman goes fishing off Cape Mudge when the wind is up, his boat may join the graveyard of boats already lost beneath the waves. The sea is more elemental, and riskier, than some of the weather concerns faced by inland farmers nowadays. Back in my grandparents' day, isolated on a Saskatchewan farm, miles from any helping hands, the weather had posed just as big a risk.

When I left Brent's house and headed to my prairie home, I carried an oyster shell in one hand, my fingers worrying the calcified ridges, following the elongated oval shape around and around. Always returning to where I had started.

THE SPIRAL
TUNNELS

A glass and metal-splinted dome in downtown Calgary curved high overhead, a black grillwork gate barring public access to the waiting line of heritage train cars, their deep burgundy bodies edged in brass and black. This was the Great Hall; the age of trains had returned.

The engineer started the engines of the Royal Canadian Pacific, and the rumble shook the foundations of the platform as I boarded, ascending through the gate at the rear of the train, lagging behind a middle-aged couple as they paused on the vestibule to bill and coo, posing for a photograph. The long-faced young man on the station holding the camera looked a lot like her—maybe he was her son? Maybe this was a second honeymoon. Or a first. Great. Lovers. Just what I needed in my current slightly bitter, single state, to witness lovers in the early bloom. My champagne splashed from its flute as the train whistle reverberated down the hall. Departure. And no one to see me off.

I chided myself for whining as we eased out of the city core and headed west, rolling sedately along the tracks and sidings adjacent to the Calgary Tower. The wheels squealed and rumbled as we gained speed and cleared downtown. At the west, we met the Bow River and rolled along its south bank. The aspen trees along the river were still dressed in summer green, although some gold filtered through on this mild September morning. En route to my stateroom, I whistled—off-key and out of tune—every train song I could think of. Hank Williams, Johnny Cash, Muddy Waters, Curtis Mayfield, Gordon Lightfoot, Pete Seeger.

I was on board on a magazine writing assignment, assessing the food and wine of a train long famed for its gourmet service. My stateroom was in a car named for N.R. Crump, a long-dead past prez of the train company, a Dickensian name, maybe, but there was no joke in the design of this compact space, as snug as a well-designed yacht, boasting a window that ran the length of my bed. The perfect spot for lounging while watching the countryside unspool beyond the glass. This was where I would hide when I could no longer endure the company of my travelling companions. Leaving my luggage on my bed to hold the crankier of my thoughts, I ducked back into the narrow corridor and went exploring.

The train sped up, and my body settled into the sideways lurches that would punctuate the rattle-and-roll rhythm of life on-board. I was grateful for my practical flat shoes, and for the shawl over my shoulder as a hedge against the breeze. Here on the eastern slopes of the Rocky Mountains, the prevailing chinook westerly wind was infamous for raising or dropping the temperature by a dozen degrees in the space of several hours. Changeability, not constancy. Like many people. I'd learned both lessons the hard way.

Wandering behind the steward for the length of the train, I paused at the open-air vestibules between each, nature in close proximity just beyond the grillwork, rattling past beneath my feet under the shifting grate.

It's a definitive moment on a train, stepping from car to car through those open-air vestibules, your foot suspended in mid-air. Sliding metal plates shift beneath you as one hand reaches from one handrail to the next, chill air across your face, grasping at the unseen, the unplanned-for. The risks we take every day, stepping across the divide, moving with hope from loss into grace, one moving car to the next. Beneath us, life whizzing by too quickly to measure or notice.

I'd left my sons behind in Calgary, and wouldn't see them or hear from them for the duration of this trip. They were almost adults, with girlfriends, jobs, lives that didn't include me on a daily basis. When they were small, they'd turned to me for every need, from pool volleyball and soccer rides to snacks after school and supper. Their moving out as young adults nearly broke my heart. I hadn't expected that visceral crack each morning when I woke and still wanted to smell their warm little-child bodies, the goodness of their sweat. "Away" was what this train trip represented, a chance to step outside my daily life, to recover or at least repair my lost and broken maternal heart.

We chugged along the narrow valley floor, leaving behind Calgary's bustling skyline dotted with construction cranes. As we swung north, I waved to my little yellow *bijou-boite* house where it perched close to the river and the train tracks in beautiful small-town Bowness, on the city's western edge. Trains marked the measure of my days in that place: my house vibrated and pots hanging from the pot rack rattled when the trains passed. Their baritone coaxed my puppy to sleep, tangled my dreams with their soothing rumble.

≈

Not since I was sixteen had I ridden on a Canadian train. Then, still living with my own mother and father on the farm—the farm I didn't yet know I'd return to at age fifty-two!—I'd headed to Vancouver from Saskatoon, alone, during Easter break to visit my elder sister, Lee. I'd eaten my lunch from a brown paper bag and slept sitting upright, curled surreptitiously against my stolid neighbour until she'd shaken herself awake in New Westminster. Lee had met me at the Vancouver terminus. "Did anything happen?" she'd asked, not wanting me to say if anything really had. I'd shaken my head. When I went home two weeks later, my father, greeting me in dead of night at the Saskatoon station, didn't ask. So I didn't tell about the crew-cut army platoon in fatigues that boarded in Edmonton and disembarked a couple hours later in Wainwright, one of them groping me under the blanket on the endless ride across the flatland, his buddies snickering in the darkness on either side of us.

≈

The Canadian Pacific Railway is a famous railroading company. Its tracks are part of a political and economic legacy dating back more than a century, an intimate and sometimes impersonal interweaving of the history and settlement of western Canada. The trains and the tracks forged the beginnings of a policy that would attempt to rid the region of its First Nations stewards before claiming large tracts of that land itself. Politics drove Prime Minister Sir John A. Macdonald's quest for a railroad through the Rocky Mountains: his vaunted "National Policy," proclaimed as British Columbia joined Confederation in 1871, explicitly aimed to support eastern manufacturing

interests, settle the west, and connect the two via a transcontinental, all-Canadian railroad. A few years later, in 1877, in what
would become Alberta in 1905, the final treaty between Canada and the Plains First Nations was signed—Treaty Seven.

Under its terms, the five signatory First Nations ceded over
130,000 square kilometres of land, from the Rocky Mountains
east to the Cypress Hills, from the Red Deer River southward
to the American border. When that land and the rest of the
prairies was divided into the tidy grid system of townships—
each a six-square-mile block—that the federal government
favoured, almost half of each township went to the railroad to
offset the expense of laying track. The imposition of the grid
system instead of the already-established Métis river lot system was a primary cause of the Métis's Northwest Resistance
of 1885—ironically, the same year that the CPR's Last Spike was
driven at Craigellachie, in Eagle Pass.

Politics aside, the Canadian railroad system achieved
world pre-eminence for its fine regional cuisine, mandated by
its gourmet "railway general," William Cornelius Van Horne,
in a bid to gain sophisticated travellers from Europe and Asia.
Van Horne proved prophetic. "If we cannot export the scenery,
we will import the tourists," he said, and he was right.[1] His art
deco–style ad campaign of posters attracted visitors into the
Rockies in phenomenal numbers—via rail, of course—to hike,
fish, and sightsee from the comfort of Canadian Pacific's baro-
nial mountain hotels.

The current incarnation of the CPR began several decades
ago, as a luxury liner that travels in circles instead of to and
from the coast. Fine regional fare continues to be a major
card in the deck, although at a vastly steeper cost than in Van
Horne's day. During the 1880s and 1890s, a train traveller riding from Winnipeg to Medicine Hat could expect to consume
eight courses from a total of thirty-five dishes at luncheon, at a

sum cost of seventy-five cents. Pierre and Janet Berton, writing in their eponymous *Canadian Food Guide*, first published in 1966, said, "If there is a distinctively Canadian style of cuisine, it is this [train cuisine]; and not too surprising that, in an artificial nation bound together by bands of steel, it should spring directly from our [railway] dining cars."[2]

≈

This sleek fleet of cars I found myself in, all made between 1917 and 1930, was pulled by a snub-nosed pair of locomotives, circa 1950. The fleet was fit for a queen, and had hosted royalty, as the "Royal" nomenclature of several cars attested. Luxurious interiors gleamed, finished in Circassian oak inlaid with bird's-eye maple, draped in Turkish fabrics, illuminated by scallop-edged lamps. Among the lovely old cars were several lounges and reading nooks, and Churchill's Cubby, a cozy corner table ideal for hosting a hand of whist. All the nooks, crannies, and cubbies were signposts to that perfect blend of camaraderie and privacy that underlaid a good vacation, and the intimate splendour of 1920s-era Pullman-style cars tried to coax me into cheerfulness. On my initial stroll, I marked out the best nooks for future retreats. There'd be time to read. Time to daydream. Time to nap. And, if the urge arrived, time to chat. On a train trip, time was the preferred currency.

That day, though, as we headed for Sicamous, across the Great Divide, I spent much of my time outdoors, absorbing the late-season sun, in a chair with my feet propped up on the wrought-iron gate of the vestibule of the Mount Stephen day-car, the last car on the train. Over the course of the trip, this spot would become a favourite haunt for two of us: me, and a former train engineer. We would meet there each morning, coffee in hand, and I would be repeatedly drawn back to its serenity after lunch and dinner. I would only rarely be alone on the vestibule, and I'd retain only a few memories of words or conversation, from my seat there or from anywhere on this trip, syllables and meanings torn from my recollection as if by the wind. I'd be left with the soundtrack of steel wheels on rails, the mournful train whistle looping back over the cars from the engine and the wind.

Book forgotten on my lap, I tipped my seat back against the wall and crossed my ankles where they sat atop the vestibule's enclosure. Framed by the grillwork of the gate, there on the rear vestibule with the receding view of train tracks, I could almost see a long lonely whistle as it trailed by, sky-long. The light and the swell of an inward-looking stone tunnel's curved face receded behind me.

≈

The steward made his appearance, calling me to lunch. Although I didn't know it yet, this train's inhalations and exhalations, the swelling call of the whistle, the rattle of the wheels, all kept time to the cooks and their long hours of effort, just as my own life as a chef had. Treading close on the steward's heels, I peered through the heated pass-through window to observe the tidily orchestrated movements of the cooks in the galley.

For lunch, as for each meal they prepared, Chef and his sous-chef smoothly worked in a pair of tightly quartered galley kitchens, two-stepping around each other, no cue-words needed. It was a tidy, self-contained workspace: cups slotted into drawers; wall shelves with lips to contain contents around curves. Faced with such regimented order, I found myself wishing for categorization in the chaos my own life had become. Where could I file this sense of loss? How to lessen the rattle of this need to belong?

Lunch seating was unassigned. The train wasn't crowded this trip, so over earthy cream of asparagus soup drizzled with white truffle oil, those of us on board adopted the habit of dining en masse, at one long table.

True to my hunch as I'd boarded, I sat across from a couple on their second honeymoon. Texans, their gulf drawl marked them as Southerners, and their conversation revealed them as train buffs who had spent nearly every holiday riding trains through Europe and Asia. They had just celebrated their twenty-fifth anniversary, and I envied them that—a milestone to share, and something I would never see. Even if I ever did remarry.

The steward was serving dessert as I finished telling them about my twenty-first birthday trip through Europe on the high-speed TGV, passing through the frozen winter hostel of Hanover en route to Vienna, my destination, home of the Lipizzaner stallions I'd travelled across the ocean and continent to see. When I'd seen the empty box stalls and learned that the horses were at Piber, their stud farm located 230 kilometres south, I'd left the stables half-blinded by tears. A middle-aged matron had adopted me as I wandered through Vienna, her young son and daughter sitting beside me on the streetcar, naming the streets and buildings in accented English. Their mother had directed me to a hostel and pointed to a good restaurant that served schnitzel, given me a ticket to see *The Nutcracker* at the Vienna State Opera, patted my arm, reminded me to eat, to call my family. Decades ago. So many years since I'd thought of that trip, and the memory of it reminded me of how rash a young woman I'd been. In later years, when I became the mother of two sons, I would surely have said "No!" if either one of them had suggested a pan-European train trip at age twenty-one, alone in deep winter. Despite the kindness of strangers I had experienced myself on a similar trip.

The meal culminated with fig and vanilla custard tart with a splash of ratafia, fortified plum spirits, as we approached Kicking Horse Pass, and the Spiral Tunnels beyond. High above the valley floor, I could see steep cement abutments, pillars as yet unfinished, for a new highway that would soar above the landscape. A few miles later, I saw cars parked on the verge of the Trans-Canada Highway high above us, light shimmering and refracting from binoculars and telescopes as the cars' drivers and passengers peered down at our train. I would drive that new stretch of highway two years hence, my goddaughter nonchalantly fiddling with my iPod in the front seat beside me; I would clench my teeth and ignore the flood of vertigo and my fear of falling from that high ribbon into the waiting Kicking Horse River far below, the tunnels buried out of sight beneath the rocks. But that day on board the train, the unfinished cement columns still reached toward the sky. Then the first tunnel opened before us, and we slipped into darkness.

≈

When Van Horne and Macdonald were shouldering the transcontinental train tracks into existence as part of a deal to drag British Columbia into Confederation, time had pressured the builders to run a very steep grade, known as the Big Hill, in order to descend a thousand feet from Wapta Lake, at the top of the Great Divide, westward to Field. After numerous fatal train crashes, uphill spur lines—like runaway lanes for out-of-control semi-trailers—were built at each end, with the switches set to open, so the engineer always had an out, escape hatches for the unlucky whose engines burned out of control on the downward run.

The current Trans-Canada Highway followed the path of the Big Hill. On driving trips to and from the coast, I'd often been caught behind a long line of motorhomes, sweltering and grinding up the long grade, or freewheeling, swerving in the omnipresent wind, on their descent.

The CPR's ultimate solution to the steepness of the grade was a pair of circular tunnels that bored directly under the tons of rocks that are Cathedral Mountain and Mount Ogden, each tunnel circling and doubling over itself with a total change in elevation of seventeen and fifteen metres respectively. In between the two tunnels, the tracks loop back and forth. It's an astonishing engineering feat, and even though I have stood at the highway's viewing post a dozen times, I never get over it—one train visible in three spots simultaneously, in and out of the tunnels, changing course and elevation as effortlessly as the river in its shale bed at the top of the Great Divide.

With the smooth plum spirits at my lips still carrying the aroma of some farmer's far-off but unforgotten plum trees, we emerged unscathed from the first tunnel. As we left the second behind, I thought about my sons. They were growing up into their own lives and orbits. It startled me to realize how we so often travel in circles, sometimes seemingly away from what we want. How the course of life is so often determined by implacable, sometimes invisible, hardships. How the track vanishes from our perception from time to time, when we proceed on faith alone, surrendering to the unseen.

Viewed from the vestibule, the Kicking Horse River tumbled through narrow racing gorges as we navigated rock cuts. The afternoon slipped by like the landscape. I put my feet up and stay put, sipping wine, chatting with the former employee of the line who also loved the view from the vestibule. This retired engineer now rode the rails for pleasure. He was built on a single-gauge plan, track-narrow shoulders and hips, his lanky arms and legs somehow evoking railway ties and stone cuts. I told him about whistling train songs when I'd boarded, and my comment triggered what would become our daily pastime, our voices wavering into the sky as we would sing every train song either of us knew, his shaky tenor supporting my contralto whenever the words stuck in my memory.

We were halted on a siding and halfway through "Canadian Railroad Trilogy" when we waved to the blue and white Rocky Mountaineer, eastbound on the same tracks we'd briefly cleared, the first of several times we would see this rival train.

"*That's* not a real train," the engineer interrupted, his nose twitching. "That's just for the tourists. Now this," and he patted the vestibule's wrought-iron grating, "this is a *train*." He was so convincing that I didn't bother reminding him that the train we were aboard had become a tourist train, too, leading travellers in circles rather than to destinations.

A couple hours later, the air changed, becoming mild and soft as we slid into the Craigellachie dining car for a late-afternoon cheese and wine tasting. I chose crystalline three-year-old cheddar, and stone-flint unoaked chardonnay, perfect for the rock-endowed landscape we were traversing, then retreated to the vestibule with the last of my wine just as the chief of the train came through the dining room, suggesting we look closely at the river.

Along the twisting turns of the Kicking Horse River, I saw up close the red-bellied kokanee salmon, a landlocked variety of sockeye, leaping in the autumn riverbed. Bald eagles perched patiently on deadwood, waiting for the perfect chance to unfurl wings and fall down the wind to snag their own meal. I'd driven the Trans-Canada Highway through the Rocky Mountains dozens of times, so I thought I'd known what to expect on this trip, but with a top speed of sixty-five miles per hour, the pace of a train was different. So was the scenery: the valley floor where the train threaded along its tracks was more personal than the four-lane highway high above us.

I waved off the steward's call to dinner and sat alone on the vestibule until we came to rest on a siding on the edges of Golden. This was where we would pass the night. An hour passed, then another, before the old trainman returned and nodded when he saw me. "You were smart," he said, rubbing his belly, his nut-brown face crinkling with a wry look that blended regret and pleasure. "Too much wine and fancy food for me." When the steward worked his way to our perch, though, tray and bottles rattling on his tidy cart, the old engineer succumbed to a splash of brandy. "Medicinal," he said, almost apologetic when I looked sideways at his wrinkled hand holding the snifter. A wave to the steward brought me a glass of the same. We sat without talking, waiting for coyotes, or owls, but the evening air was uninterrupted, glossed over by stars and a minimalist moon. It was after midnight before I crawled into my narrow bed, spawning salmon swimming through my dreams, and although the train was stationary, I felt the rocking of the wheels all night as I slept.

In the morning, before the other guests and most of the staff were up and about, I took myself for a walk down the narrow corridor. I heard the rumble of metal on metal in low timbre, some minor key I could not name, like a cat purring or a son singing a morning pavane. When the train abruptly began to move, I lurched, the walls playing pinball with my shoulder, the smooth weave of fabric pattern and palm prints along the window and the wall as I swayed from wall to wall with the rhythm of the wheels. I wanted my life on balance, as collected as the servers and cooks on this topsy-turvy train.

I slipped to the lounge between the dining room and the Churchill Cubby, the only spot on this miracle of compact design spacious enough for my yoga mat. By the time my sun salutation was done, the sun was up. Coffee, a stroll the length of the eleven shining railcars, each over eighty feet long, back to the rear vestibule to sketch wild flowers, ink memories of the Selkirk and Monashee mountainsides' valley vegetation. Beyond the blossoms, spawning salmon turned Mission Creek into a sea of red bodies.

The train rolled to a halt in Sicamous, against a backdrop of lazy houseboats and tree-lined lakeshore, and we disembarked. We would rejoin it in Kamloops, desert country, after a day-trip by bus carried us down half the length of Okanagan Lake. When I asked why we switched to a bus, our hostess told us that the train could take the track south, but passage would be slow. She was right, if road traffic speed was similar to train speeds in such a narrow, winding valley. We rolled alongside Mara Lake, then Okanagan Lake, all the way to Enderby, an emerging wine region blessed with peaches and beaches. Throughout the Okanagan, from its cool-climate north end to the sun-baked desert of Osoyoos, wineries have proliferated, some driving out peach and apple orchards.

At an orchard in Vernon, I giggled as we boarded little wagons bolted behind a tractor, recalling my sons as little boys, their long-since-changed voices shrieking with laughter in my head as we toured fifty acres of trees, ripe fruit hanging heavy. We returned to the shop to taste apple varieties, the snap and sparkle of Ambrosia, Fuji, Mutsu, and early Jersey Macs, then more eating—apple pie in a resplendently tender crust, with generous scoops of ice cream—on the sunny deck. It was surprisingly easy to drift into a nap as the bus retreated north-ward, up the valley and across the hills, through the scrubby desert to Kamloops. Dinner on our return to the train was all-Albertan: tender steak with caramelized shallots, partnered by glasses of surprisingly fine Okanagan red. When I got to bed, I dreamed of red-glazed gears and wheels within wheels, smok-ing and swimming in wine.

Next morning, I stepped on the vestibule and looked east, up the track where we were spotted. "Spotted?" I'd said in confusion when the old engineer had first used the term. He'd laughed, explaining that to railroaders, the word meant "parked," but on a siding, not in a yard. His explanation echoed in my head as I ran back up the corridor for my camera to record the sunrise gleaming along the length of the glittering tracks and gleaming sides of the stationary cars. After my con-stitutional—coffee on the vestibule, a stroll around the spot-ted train to look for flowers, then breakfast—the train growled into wakefulness and we departed Kamloops, heading east, back toward the mountains, and Calgary.

≈

The evening's entertainment was a champagne-focused din-ner, with a classical music duo to follow. During dinner, the sommelier opened bottles of premium champagnes like a man committed to bubble art—a Krug magnum, Ruinart R de Ruinart, Billecart, Perrier-Jouët *grand brut*. Champagnes I'd heard of but had not tried before. Chef riposted with sautéed scallops, onion soup, fennel-crusted lamb loin, a chocolate extravaganza.

Afterward, we staggered into the Mount Stephen car as if we'd been drugged, and a couple of us jigged and jived, our dinner hanging full and weighty in our bellies. Tomorrow we would return to Calgary. Later, as I traversed from car to car, I felt as if I had always slept on a train, had spent my entire life in the rolling gait of a Maritimer.

On our final day, we climbed from Golden into the mountains, back across a trestle bridge, through stone-cut tunnels, east along the tracks that took us west a few days ago. I barely noticed this time as the cars shuttled through the Spiral Tunnels, then down to the valley bottom again, to where the salmon and eagles were still haunting the rivers, and the air still felt like late summer. I carried my glass out to the vestibule, anxious to harbour the vestiges of this trip, equally anxious to see my family. My pique and moody depression had faded into the whistle steam.

We rolled along the amber prairie immediately west of Calgary, and the skyline was no longer Douglas fir or lodgepole pine, but skyscraper and steel. We disembarked in the Great Hall, staggered a bit at the sense of solid earth instead of moving platform, and waved goodbye to the stalwart steel horse. I wish I could report that as I glanced around the terminal, I spotted them, both my sons, tall against the sky, waving to me. Welcoming me home. But they were not there. I went home on my own, and it took me years to accept the lesson with grace—that my sons had become adults and had embarked on their own travels.

ANNUAL
CANNING BEE

One evening, when both my sons fill my small home with their enthusiasms, they throw open my fridge and rummage for condiments as supper approaches. There is nothing new about their behaviour. My sons are accustomed to full shelves and bursting fridges. They love pickles, relishes, jams, and mustards of all sorts, and are accustomed to homemade. They grew up in a 1950s-era Calgary bungalow with an uninsulated "cold room" tucked into a corner of the basement. In spite of its small size and its narrow squeeze-through shape, its crowded shelves were the core of the house. Jars stood in lines and groups, the gold, the jewellery, the cascades of seasonal riches, all the bright warm breath of summer captured to colour the pallid plates of winter.

I have no cold room in this older, smaller home, but my sons and I remember.

≈

This row here, this translucent purple, this row is the memory of my youngest son making beet pickles, ladling brine and purple vegetables, stirring, intent mouth pursed in concentration. "Like this, Mom?" he asked as he wiped the rim.

"Just like that, my darling," I answered as I filed the moment in my living archive.

And here, this fragrant, tinted applesauce, and this pineapple and peach chutney, full of the late autumn sunshine that shone on my friend Phyllis and me, a light that barely warmed the skins of my goddaughters as we wrapped our sweaters about them, shivering in the innocent windy cold. We were at the annual late-season produce sale, the wooden ways crowded with crates, boxes, and bins, tents and marquees strung across the roadway. Heaps of peppers and peaches, acres of ripe apples, russet pears in Botticelli curves, all selling at ancient prices. Each year, we would wander in amazement, wondering at the true worth of a dime or a nickel.

"A case of apples!" Phyllis said when we spotted the new-crop Galas and Gravensteins. A box went into our wagon, and we threaded slowly through the crowds.

At the next tent, I spotted late-season peaches, remembered standing in the dry desert air of Cawston in the Similkameen valley, in a farmer's orchard eating a perfect peach, its juices running into my tears.

"Let's split a case," I said. Phyllis nodded. "I have lots of fresh ginger. If we buy peaches, we'll make chutney together." Love and sun are all blended together with the juice of peach and the bite of ginger.

≈

This black currant jam is from Mom's patch of berries, tinged with the bitterness of her failed palate, her taste buds gone to rest before the rest of her body, her life's enjoyment of scents and tastes wrested from her unasked. The currants, hand-picked beneath the hot prairie sun, black and dusky, are musky and slightly soft beneath my mother's worn brown fingers. The jam, near black, is flavoured with her sadness.

The chili sauce—red last year, a decade ago tinged a warm and vibrant orange when I bought a case of orange heirloom tomatoes, and once, sunny from yellow Brandywines—this one is my southern Ontarian paternal grandmother's mother's mother's, the recipe passed to me and now my own, tinkered with and adapted to my liking. My grandmother with her dark-red hair hid her temper under her smile and never showed it under stress. The secret child's life of my father is gone with her, but my sons treasure the memory of their great-grandmother each time they open a jar of chili sauce.

My sons want chili sauce to tuck inside their supper omelettes, but there is none until the tomatoes are ripe at the market. "Mom, let's fill the shelves, you're out of preserves," they chorus. "We want to can with you this year."

This year my sons and I will go to the annual harvest sale together. Dailyn will pull the wagon as his brother Darl stacks cases of fruit onto it. Then we will cook together. Memories, waiting to be made.

FLOODPLAIN

"Here lies one whose name was writ in water."

~ THE EPITAPH OF POET JOHN KEATS

R hekia called on 22 June 2013. "Helicopters. They've sent out helicopters to make evacuation announcements," she said. Her voice was thin, rushing, tipping into panic. "Everyone in Bowness has to get out."

I could make out the thrum of 'copter blades when she stopped speaking. I'd been following the news, knew the Bow and Elbow Rivers flowing into Calgary were running high, that rain was setting new records. Rhekia and my eldest son, Darl, lived in the old west-side Calgary neighbourhood of Bowness, where they rented my elderly house, a block uphill from the Bow. Uphill.

"How will you get out?" I asked, trying to grasp the subtext of what she was saying.

"Dailyn's here with his car. We've got forty-five minutes before they close the bridges. We can't take the cats."

"Where are you going?"

"My dad's. Darl's still at work. I can't reach him."

≈

It's uneasy, my relationship with water. Filled with mistrust. Put me into a canoe, a rowboat, sailboat, or cruise ship, and my innards instantly rebel against the movement and make every effort to break loose for shore. I don't rock myself to sleep as if still in the womb, snug in my mother's aqueous pond. Don't dream of life beside the ocean's restless pulse of tide.

I don't blame my experiences, although some have been traumatic. At thirteen, in the pool of Girl Guides camp. The deep end. My leap had been voluntary despite my so-so swimming ability, a futile attempt to fit in with girls I didn't know and would never see again after this two-week stint of hiking and mosquitoes and smoke in my hair and clothing. If camp was hell, nearly drowning was the seventh circle, violence, fiery flakes igniting my chest as I struggled, head below the surface, arms flailing to find the side of the pool. My lungs were alight by the time some faceless counsellor, all arms and comforting hands, pulled me out of the water.

I learned to swim for real in my early twenties, impelled by a desire to scuba dive. I grew to love unfolding lengths in Vancouver Aquatic Centre's fifty-metre salt-water pool, the stretch and glide of my arms, my body arrowing through the water back and forth, fingers tagging the end of the pool on each pass. And years later, pregnant, uncomfortably waiting for my first baby's birth in the midst of an overheated Calgary summer, I would take daily refuge in the YWCA's swimming pool, at ease in my skin again, my baby-bump belly tipping me from side to side as my guppy rolled.

But lanes and buoys didn't prepare me for open-water dives. At twenty-two, scuba diving in zero visibility off the west coast of Vancouver Island, an inlet gushing with spring runoff and plankton bloom. We held hands and went down, almost blind, into murky greenness. Panic started before we descended five feet, my chest refusing to open and close in time with the regulator clenched between my teeth. I groped my way up my diving buddy's arm, found his hand, shaped the thumb upward: surface.

My New Age friends laugh, calling me a classic cardinal earth sign. Capricorns aren't meant to be sailors. We're the gardeners of the planet. Dirt, mud, dust—these are our friends. We like boots. We welcome water—as rain, urging our Brandywine tomato seeds into embodiment. As the mystery of mist. In gutters and rain pipes and pooling on windowpanes, rushing along downspout into rain barrels and buckets. And yes, even as waves, admired from a respectful distance. Nothing more intimate.

≈

A week passed before the city cleared Bowness district to returning residents. Rhekia and Darl moved back into the house as soon as the bridges opened; then Rhekia called to fill me in. The power had been turned off in their absence and the food in the fridge had spoiled, she said, the stink of waste haunting fridge and freezer. Both cats were fine.

"I did a walk-around of the house, and a basement wall is bulging," she reported.

"What do you mean, bulging?"

"Bulging. Like it's pregnant."

"Which wall? Send me a picture."

What she emailed didn't help. I packed a bag.

≈

The night before I drove to Calgary from our acreage near Saskatoon, I dreamed, a nightmare limned in red. Three scarlet points, my liver lit up, a Christmas tree, some unlikely phosphorescent test, a mad student's imagination run amok. Flickering carmine, crimson, cardinal. Liver, gall bladder, kidney. Liver: house of the spirit. Gall bladder: outpost of meditation or calm. Kidney: mirror of desire. In my dream, I placed a layer of parchment over the desired outcome. Rubbed it into a smudge. Ignited incense. As I inhaled cedar and jasmine, I remembered coastal dogwood trees alight with redheaded woodpeckers, the nearby current teasing their wandering souls and housebound bills. Bills. Beaks. Red blood on a napkin blooming from my son's bruised forehead. Skateboard wheels. Dealers wielding half-naked girls as status symbols, my son intoxicated by what he could not have. Red points blossoming into firewater that dripped downward from shingles and eavestroughing.

≈

When I woke, a pelican like a tall ship under sails christened the surface of the lake at my doorstep. A first, and unusual. What pelican shelters on a lake? What makes a lake a lake, disparate from the mudflat sound of *slough*? Volume of water? Amount of homeland displaced? Acreage of beachfront property? Docks cartage decks quays piers wharfs harbours? Quality of vegetation? Degree of cattails winning over sedge? The pelican unfurled her mizzenmast: all day as I headed west, I was haunted by "The Wreck of the Edmund Fitzgerald."

The elephant in the room was the fact I'd already endured one flood: my Saskatchewan land had been flooded two years earlier. Not by a river, but by snow melt after a record-breaking snowfall and a previous summer of unprecedented rain. On the long highway to Calgary, my mind tussled and wrestled with the elephant's trunk: what does water mean?

≈

Calgary was beginning to emerge from its worst-ever inundation. Before I'd hopped in the car for the drive west, photographs posted online had showed the Saddledome, the indoor stadium in Calgary's famed Stampede Park, tiers deep in water. Downtown streets flowed away. Prince's Island Park, the inner-city pastoral jewel in the middle of the Bow River, was completely swamped. The civic zoo, on adjacent St. George's Island, posted pictures of giraffes in belly-deep water. Riverfront properties, once prime real estate, were shoulder-deep in sludge and waste. My favourite footbridge across the Elbow River was destroyed and blockaded from use, cables and twisted metal holding the wreckage to one bank. Volunteers were stepping in everywhere, shovelling mud, cooking, hauling away ruined furniture. Downstream, the entire town of High River became a disaster zone. My small house's small bulging wall on the west side of Calgary seemed like a tiny issue in what had become an enormous province-wide problem.

≈

It was raining when I arrived in Calgary. Along Memorial Drive beside the Bow River, dogs retreated, their tails whipping screen doors into lather, cats in hiding under maples, trucks, fallen trees. The river, high and brown, littered with flotsam, snarled a new path to cracking foundations, shifting joists, growing breaches. Soloing cornet above the river, a goose blew Armstrong, Beiderbecke, plangent notes twanging back from a metal sky. A too-sharp guitar string. A kazoo. It was easy to imagine that note spiralling into space, nothing to restrain it, not refracting until it encountered the Milky Way, asteroid belt, Jupiter's rings, comets circling, drawn by the calling goose.

The cats twined around my legs when I stepped onto the deck at my old house. I hugged Rhekia, picked up Elsie the kitten and scratched her chin as Rhekia led me onto the street and pointed at the train tracks a hundred yards west of the house.

"Look. Before we left, water was running down the slope of the cul-de-sac from the train tracks," Rhekia said. "Huge puddles. The trains sprayed water across the tracks in front of them."

Downstairs, the floor was dry, Darl's computer gear and musical instruments still safely stacked on tables and couches, metal rattling on metal as a train chugged past.

As Rhekia pointed out the cracks spidering upward, the shift in the ceiling, the widening gaps, I remembered that a few years ago I had crossed a footbridge into Beaumont Park, the natural area that meanders along the north shore of the Bow River a block away. At the apex of the small bridge, I'd stopped and dropped a clutch of roses and larkspur into the busy glacial water, my way of saying goodbye again to a young girl, a schoolmate of my youngest son, Dailyn. She'd drowned one spring as she walked home alone late one night after visiting her boyfriend on the north side, then crossed the Bow River in full spate from mountain runoff. I reimagined the treacherous footbridge, her family, torn loose from land as we are torn from sleep each morning, leaving railing and shore, like the night, in tatters.

"Look," Rhekia said again, pointed to the cracking ceiling, the bulging wall. All I saw were green tidal pools, plaster metamorphosing into late-spring ice. "We need to bring in an expert."

≈

The structural engineer was absolute. "It's unsafe," he said as he squatted and studied the carnage the next morning. He'd made us take a knife to the basement wall: we'd slit open dry-wall to reveal a belly of stones like entrails that spilled onto the floor as a body does after an injury. Rotting insulation. Two-by-fours like cardboard. "There's no wall."

"No wall?" I must have sounded like a mindless echo. "What do you mean, no wall?"

We gaped and looked closer. Two-by-fours slowly failing. No support structure. No concrete. No pressure-treated wood. No beams. Some previous owner, looking for ways to shave costs from his addition, had thrown up a fake wall of nothing more substantial than dreams, slapped wallboard on top, and painted it over.

"Your family can't stay here," the engineer said. His voice thickened with sympathy. "I don't know precisely when, but this house will come down."

What had been a tiny bulge, a small problem, suddenly, monstrously, bloomed into an unexpected disaster of unknown dimensions.

≈

At home, I often wake to morning mist on the lake, our umbrel-la above the picnic table the only clear-cut outline. The ruins of history in all those drowned cars and farm machines that litter the field—rows and rows of wrecks abandoned by my brothers, my dad, my grandfather—are softened by fog. Gran sweating in the grain truck, late summer heat wavering around her, waiting for amber wheat to pool in the box from the combine's spitting mouth. The green Mercury we'd ridden in to check the mailbox at the corner, a particular aroma of heat captured in its dusty upholstery. The flatbed of the pickup truck my brothers and I had clumsily stacked with hay bales as we'd learned how to live like farmers when we'd arrived, unwillingly relocated by our parents in the early 1970s. The hours I'd spent as a teenager wandering the fields and bush on my horse, daydreaming myself into the artist's life I wanted. The flood-lake has become a bank where we store what we cannot bear to hold or recall. In time, the locks rust and all we have are those outlines in the mist, dull edges we can't keep honed sharp and bright. What memories I polish and sharpen are chrome-shiny, the rust yet to settle.

≈

Rhekia bent her head to her phone after the engineer took his leave. A few minutes later, she raised her eyes to mine. "There's nothing to rent. Nothing we can afford. This city's gone crazy with the flood. All the rentals are suddenly astronomical."

She and both my boys were cooks. Cooks' wages don't stretch to flood-jacked rents.

≈

I want to talk to rain after a flood. To describe skin, pelts punished by raindrops like fists and hypodermics, pounded as a junkie pounds his own body, punctuating with needles that pierce what cannot be broken with fists. To describe a river, swollen as if deep-kissed by a lover for eons. Swollen as if stung by an errant hive of bees that mistook it for flowers so flowing with nectar they couldn't resist kissing it to death.

≈

While Rhekia called Darl at work, I walked the short block north to Bow Crescent and turned east toward the house of my friends Phyllis and Randy, set back from the river's edge, up on a long sloping yard. Only the first ten feet of yard closest to the bank had been invaded by the river.

Phyllis was at her sewing desk. "Dee! What are you doing in town? What a nice surprise!" Before she opened her arms, I started to sob.

Recounting the story took a while. Phyl put her hand on my arm. "It's fate," she said. When I looked at her in surprise, she went on. "Fate. Lise and her boyfriend are moving to London. The basement suite will be available in a couple weeks. Tell Darl and Rhekia to come look. They can put their stuff in the garage until then."

≈

Riding a borrowed horse behind a mile-long dam in central Saskatchewan in 2011, Diefenbaker Lake stretching on the other side, all I could imagine was the breakthrough. Being swept away. Losing control. An orgasm of immeasurable proportions. I shrugged my shoulders together under the weight of sky masquerading as ponds of light, nudged the horse into a canter, raced for the far end of the dam.

≈

Water is light, mirror-glass physics, angle of incidence equals angle of refraction. Is mercury droplets. A sheet. Ice/steam/fluid. Invisible. A rock-chipped diamond. A skater's agony. A skier's liftoff above the T-bar. Raft supporter, life raft. Float. Inhale, and death to all but fish. Life and death. Water is blue green aqua emerald azure cobalt sapphire cerulean indigo. Sea of Tranquility. Sea of despond. Sea of heartache. Water is in. Out. Fashionable bottles, stored, iced, jugged, poured, hoarded, squandered. Water is hip. The Arctic, tamed and bottled, icebergs with olives and a twist. Tankers, plastic bottles forming floating islands of post-industrial despair in the oceans. Glasses. A mattress. Water is eternal. Evanescent. A desert. An ocean.

≈

We moved Darl and Rhekia's belongings in one afternoon, a conga line of trucks, SUVs, and cars threading the streets to Phyl and Randy's garage. My son and his partner packed crates, boxes, and suitcases snugly into the garage's dim space while I stood in the middle of my house a block away, feeling betrayed, the house's broken ribs wheezing around me. I'd thought for years that this tiny yellow-skinned house would be my final residence, my rabbit bolt-hole and my shelter when I was alone again.

Rhekia came in, sweating, relatively calm, her phone in her hand. "Darl's dad is going to let us stay at his condo until he comes back into town," she said. "By then, Lise and her partner will be moved to London. It's all worked out fine."

But it hasn't. I wanted to cry.

≈

It hasn't. Water is an uninvited guest in a place of drowning. A place of myths. Swords and a woman's samite-clothed arm, sword returned to the cauldron of water, giving the mythical King Arthur a chance of immortality and redemption. I'm still waiting on redemption.

Despite all our failings, despite its power to sweep us into the brink, into the unknown, water is the deepness within that is our harbour, that harbours also the secrets we cannot share. Vile, bloody, or deceitful, unfulfilled secrets. Water is a place of death, of birth. Of loss. And hope, ice, melt, snow. Of soft-hearted autumn, reluctant to let go. Of spring, last at the door. Of orchids supplanted by cattails. Where muskrats dream their way through winter, where frogs burrow into mud. Water is the last refuge of the homeless trance, the one that incites, lights incendiary candles to fling at time. The one that ignites icicles upside down. The one where dancing is always an option, where riding bare-legged on horseback carries me headlong into what delights. Why beside water lovers lie. Why beneath water catfish moan. Why beside water the beggars gather for scraps of unused light. The very thing that attracts one drives away the other.

≈

I leave Darl and Rhekia to mop up and drive to a hot, sterile, stuffy office to start the soulless process of applying for governmental aid, aid that, a year later, would not be forthcoming—beyond a cheque to cover the expense of hiring the engineer. My tears drip onto the application papers as I sign my name, small foreshadow of more to come.

≈

When I drive home to Saskatchewan a day later, I return to a cup of rainfall in a stainless bowl on my sewing table, dripped from the ceiling, tiles arcing and gaping to expose subcutaneous layers of plastic and insulation, the bones visible beneath the wound. Errant drops stain the table's wood surface, darker, slick, magnifying the grain. Beside the table, my dog's water bowl is full of tap water, snubbed in favour of rainwater in an old metal kettle, my watering can for plants, his nose leading unerringly to water free of manganese, magnesium, sulphur, iron. Is it true that all the water exists now that has ever, will ever? That water is the ultimate recycling circle? From clouds to rain to ground to steam vapour to cloud to rain to watering container to dog's curling pink tongue, an exploration of loss in warmth.

Outside the house stand buckets of rainwater, three brimming rain barrels. I walk the flood-lake, looking for pond lilies to sprout and lotus blossoms to open in unexpected places, like koi dreaming of koi dreaming of me dreaming of a dream. The flood is a lake, far beyond pond-like expectations. At what point do acres of pond become lake? My soundings take out a mortgage on imaginings, bank the outcome as if they were rands or doubloons. Value ascribed to water equals what, exactly? A drop in the bucket. An echo. A sigh. A dog's wet nose.

WIEBO'S WAY

At six in the morning, a hammer-blow on my door startles me from sleep. "Breakfast in ten minutes," a low voice outside the building murmurs. Still dark outdoors. Somewhere not very far away, a coyote howls, and my skin prickles as I walk to the main house. In the kitchen, lights are on but the wood stove sits unlit, and the room is chilly. A blackboard mounted on an easel announces the meal: bread and butter, jam, hot multigrain cereal with milk and honey, red raspberry leaf tea.

Wiebo Ludwig sits at the head of the table, surrounded by his sons and daughters—almost a dozen, teenaged to mid-thirties. He points directly across from him at an empty chair as I survey the room. His wife, Mamie, rises repeatedly from her chair, keeping a close eye on her granddaughters as they set out the meal for the forty-three residents of the farm. The girls finally take seats at an adjoining table and Wiebo says a brief blessing. After a chorus of "amen," no one speaks. The brown bread is chewy, still warm, the butter sweet. The honey has traces of buckwheat in its amber depths. I pass on the hot cereal and let my tea go cold.

The air settles and stills as the chewing slows and plates and bowls empty. The children leave the table, followed by several women—I can't keep them all straight—daughters, daughters-in-law. The young men get up, leaving their dishes on the table. None leaves the room, taking up stations close by, a congregation leaning on counters and cupboards that they helped build. Mamie and several of the young grandchildren methodically pick up cutlery, glasses, plates, and cups, stacking them beside the deep sink. She puts her index finger over her lips when they start to chatter, sets them to their tasks, then comes back to the table, standing beside her husband, one hand on his shoulder. Protectively? I wonder, surprised, but after a second glance, I change my opinion: no, in solidarity.

Over the clatter of dishes and the murmur of running water, I can hear indomitable birdsong. Chickadees.

Wiebo is implacable granite. He finally shifts position to butter one more slice of bread, all the while watching me steadily. When he speaks, his voice is harsh and clipped.

"You are married?"

"Divorced," I admit.

"That is a damnable state. You have children?"

"Yes. Two sons."

"And are they happy, you being divorced?"

It's impossible to not answer. "No. They aren't. They wish we were back together again." I stumble over my words, defensive, tongue-tied, overwhelmed by his forceful but unvoiced expectation that I would reply, that I would tell the truth.

"Society is broken. It is burning its way to hell," Wiebo says calmly. "And you will go to hell with all the rest."

At this, Mamie intervenes. "She does her best for her children, I'm sure," she says, sounding like the peacekeeper in the desert.

But Wiebo isn't finished or placated. "You believe in God?"

"Oh yes," I say, glad to have at least one answer that will suit the pastor. But it doesn't help.

"Do you go to church?" At my headshake, more questions: "And you. Are you happy? In that God-forgotten society?"

To my chagrin, I answer, and truthfully. "No. Well, not really. I mean . . ." Why do I not hold my tongue? Or hold my ground? Or at least lie? I struggle to explain how I feel isolated and overworked as a recently divorced single mother, but it's too late. I see the satisfaction on his face. How could I let those words slip past the gateway when I knew he's out there waiting to ambush me?

A rant follows, long minutes on the evils of modern Western society, the breakdown of Christian values, the fiery doom awaiting all who participate. Even in my dazed and overwhelmed state, I interpret it as an attempt to bring me to my knees—or at least to humble me: he harangues me on my role as a woman and a journalist in what he characterizes again and again as a broken society. Then more about my divorce. My sons' well-being. My own state of mind. My faith—and more to the point, its absence. I should walk out. I should interrupt, answer back, defend myself. But I do none of those things.

"My job is to minister to my flock," Wiebo says eventually, drawing to a close, "even those who do not know they are of my flock."

"Amen." His sons' voices are a gospel choir of baritones, assenting and counterpointing.

He nods at me, and although I am now staring down at the tabletop, I sense his hand rising in benediction. No one speaks as I retreat from the breakfast table, feeling as broken as he has accused me of being, swallowing my tears.

≈

I arrived at Trickle Creek Ranch the day before to a warm greeting.

"Welcome," Wiebo Ludwig said. His hand as he shook mine was hard as well-aged timber. A crowd gathered around us—children, babes, adults. The children were unabashedly curious but cautious, their wide gazes from behind their mothers' skirts, the braver ones finally coming up to the stranger among them to giggle and gaze close-up, a wide-open appraisal. The young girls were bareheaded, their hair confined in braids, but the teenaged girls and older women wore scarves over their long hair, and ankle-length flowing cotton skirts. The men were bearded. It all felt biblical, and I had a sudden sense of elsewhere, and time running in reverse. Even though it was 2007, and this was Canada. The far western end of Alberta's Peace Country, granted, but still Canada.

Wiebo directed one of his sons to take my bag and himself led me to a guest room in an adjoining building, his hand on my arm. He was sixty-four, stocky and muscular, with a cropped grey beard and riveting blue eyes that looked me up and down, studying me as closely as he'd examine a piece of timber or a broodmare. He was infamous across the province and through Western Canada as a saboteur of oil and gas installations, but I was charged by a magazine with investigating his human side. The family compound's off-the-grid sustainable footprint was leading the country's alternative-living cadre: biofuels and wind turbines, straw-bale buildings and solar-heated green-house, sawmill, organically raised livestock as well as home-grown and house-milled grains, estate-produced wines, and artisanal cheeses. I was there to see how this renegade family fed themselves.

Wiebo emanated charm. With a single exhalation that felt like relief as it sank through my ribs and down to my belly, I allowed myself to succumb. While taking me walkabout, his family trailing along behind, to see the animals in their spacious barns and fields, he smiled often and patted my arm repeatedly.

"You've never seen such plenty," he said, waving at the fields, taking it as a given. "Look, see my youngest, that's Ishshah, she's my blessing. She grows all our tomatoes." He pointed to Ishshah, at sixteen still young enough to unselfconsciously drop to her knees and cuddle the newborn kids in the goats' barn. Later that evening after supper concluded, Ishshah would sit on her father's lap, and he would cradle her like a fragile and beloved doll. Still later, before the moon rose, with her sisters and mother she would shed her headscarf to dance in the field, an ancient sight, slow-moving, sensual, swaying skirts and lithe bodies that brought to mind the wind in the grain. It disturbed me, witnessing that dance: who was it for?

At the swimming dugout, a trio of grandchildren eagerly showed off their otter-like swimming style, diving off the dock, wading past the rockery border. It was a pretty spot, cool in the late afternoon light, shaded with poplar trees and bulrushes, and reminded me of my grandparents' farm in central Saskatchewan, the place where I now live.

One young grandson, as tall as his grandsire, was at the woodpile close by, swinging an axe.

"There is always work to do," Mamie said, following my eyes. "But we never hurry. If we need a nap, we go lie down. My daughters and daughters-in-law live better lives than women at work in town, and meet their children's needs more easily. Life for us is full, not just family life, but taking care holistically." She paused and looked closely at me, studying my face, my just-emerging wrinkles, I imagined. "Most people don't see what is under their very feet—their kids, the fullness of life."

Mamie, fifty-nine, was her husband's "fruitful vine," mother of eleven, grandmother of twenty-seven. Her eyes were a faded cornflower-blue, set amid a network of crow's feet that tracked years of work. She was tall, a handsome, strong-boned woman who laughed easily, making no fuss over her husband's flirting. But as I would learn the next morning, when the faith cards were played, she was his chorus.

≈

I was raised by an air force father and a steel-spined farm mother, neither of whom brooked any nonsense or naysaying from their five kids. Suffice to say that I grew up with my own share of grit: during my time as a restaurateur and chef in Calgary, I was called "the Ice Queen" behind my back. But blunt-talking men with an air of authority intimidated me. Later in life, I was glad to meet and fall in love with Dave, a gentle, cooperatively inclined human being with no need to exercise an inner junkyard guard dog. But prior to that, I had my fill of alpha males, and Wiebo Ludwig topped the list. And yes, he intimidated the hell outta me. Of course, as a convicted saboteur, he scared half of Western Canada for a couple decades, so I wasn't alone.

The story of Wiebo's sometimes-violent and highly charged battle with Big Oil is chronicled elsewhere in great detail, including Andrew Nikiforuk's Governor General's Award–winning book, *Saboteurs*. But Wiebo was also a charming, intelligent man with a gift of—what, exactly? In olden days, we'd have said "the gift of tongues," and meant it literally. Yes, as an orator and preacher, he had the gift of tongues, and he wasn't afraid to use his gift as a flail against society for all its failures. But he was also gifted with keen sight: long ahead of electric car magnates and wind farmers, Wiebo saw the future as oil-free, and he took radical steps to chivvy society toward that vision. That made for instant and unending conflict in Alberta, the provincial house that still rises and falls with oil and gas fortunes, where in times of bust, oil barons have been heard to mutter, "Just one more boom, please, and I promise I won't piss it away this time."

Wiebo's views of gender roles, family, society, and God shaped the daily functions of all the inhabitants of Trickle Creek. He was characterized in the media as difficult and stubborn, with a temper that could flare out of control. Descended from Dutch peasant stock, he imposed on his family a rigourously self-reliant life reminiscent of his nineteenth-century farming forebears. The entire farm was made by Ludwig hands, with the necessary learning in a wide range of skill sets accomplished by books and online learning, in one of those amazing contradictions that seems impossible to fathom. Quoted in the *Edmonton Sun* in 2013, his son Josh said, "People are way too intimidated today by professionalism—the idea that you have to go to school for four years to do something. We all have degrees from the University of Trickle Creek."[1] That self-directed approach resonates with me: as an autodidact, I too have learned to do many things by doing them, although not to the extreme required by the Ludwig clan.

≈

After Wiebo's interrogation, I sit on my bed in the chilly bedroom, the lamp off, feeling frozen, chastised, and painfully young, reliving moments from my childhood, when I was conditioned to acquiescence and subservience. "Be quiet, your father is sleeping!" and "You wait until your father gets home!" were the two poles of discipline my mother swung between.

I could leave the compound. I probably should. But I have a story to capture.

≈

It takes no great insight to realize that Wiebo reminds me of my father. The same imperious and unspoken insistence on a response generates automatic obedience in me; the same sense of near-overwhelming physical presence, a threat held in check by will alone, instigates near-physical fear. Has Wiebo beaten Mamie? His kids? How far does he go to enforce his belief in the primacy of men over women—that "headship" he enforces, his belief that feminine submission in all things includes the symbolic covering of women's hair?

I've never seen my dad strike my mother. In his years as a young father of five, Dad's frustration with his own life came out as yelling and intimidation, yes, and sometimes as physicality, spanking us kids with his leather belt, an accepted form of punishment in the years before such tactics became defined as assault. But Dad has never resorted to the psychological gamesmanship that is Wiebo's way. Bred in the choking stratification of gothic southern Ontario's tradition of reserve and family secrecy, my father never interrogates me about my personal life, and rarely talks about his. Never insults me about my choices and my lifestyle.

And then I wonder about my paternal grandmother, Doris, that authoritative bastion of southern Ontario society, acutely aware of status and her place in it. She was a single parent through the hard years of the Second World War while my Granddad Bill was stationed at a radar base. Dad rarely speaks of her. Had my grandmother beaten him?

I don't know. The closest I came to learning the truth of my dad's upbringing arrived a year before my trip north to Trickle Creek, as Dad and I stood nose to nose in my yard, the crab apple blossoms a cloud of disarming pink behind us. We'd spent two weeks renovating the bathroom and kitchen of my new home, a tiny one-hundred-year-old house a block off the Bow River in Calgary. The house was a bright jewel box that charmed me from my first sight, but my realtor told me I was crazy, that even at its knockdown asking price, it needed too much love to make it worth my money. I bought it anyway. Tiling the kitchen floor had been more problematic than I'd expected: the floor sloped in a downhill pitch that sent marbles rolling freely, and it had taken several days to level it before we could set a single tile in place. My patience was running thin: Dad was shooting sightlines, measuring, measuring again, pencilling measurements on the plywood we'd just screwed down. Surely we didn't have to be quite so meticulous. Watching him clamber slowly to his feet from his hands and knees yet again, his carpenter's belt loose around his hips, I suddenly realized how much he'd aged. A wire long pulled taut loosened deep within me. We went out to the garage for another box of tiles, and I turned to him. I didn't plan what came from my mouth.

"I'm not afraid of you anymore." The words hung, fluttering in the air like those crab apple blossoms. The urge to explain took over. "I've been in therapy for most of my adult life, Dad, and I've chosen some incredibly inappropriate men as partners. But I'm not afraid anymore."

His face had caved in at my words. "I just did what I knew," he said slowly, and hugged me. "I'm sorry."

≈

In my turn, although I swore to be a new kind of parent and rarely struck them, how did I fail my own sons? Especially my eldest, Darl, who at fifteen had taken his family's separation and divorce so terribly hard. First his face crumpled, and then his life, given over first to struggles at school, then to larger struggles. I have dizzy memories of moments from my deepest depression before our marriage ended, of hurling myself at my ex-husband, Don, and pounding his chest with my fists. It still shames me that I modelled such a terrible example, and it breaks my heart that Darl yearned for years to return us all to that broken family unit.

Adverse childhood experiences (ACE) is how childhood trauma is described today by addiction researcher Dr. Daniel Sumrok. On the ACEs Too High website, Sumrok is quoted as saying that "ritualized compulsive comfort-seeking (what traditionalists call addiction) is a normal response to the adversity experienced in childhood, just like bleeding is a normal response to being stabbed."[2] How to make this fact a helpful aid instead of a stigma, a fact that will help my son find peace with himself and his life? It's taken me almost two decades to learn that acceptance and forgiveness pave the way to peace, and that peace is preferable to the adrenalin-spiked high-tension wire of confrontation and conflict that defined my childhood and marriage. I am grateful to observe that my son learned more quickly than I did.

≈

By the time I emerge from my room at Trickle Creek, I have mopped up my tears. But I'm sure Mamie can see their traces. Her husband is nowhere in sight.

With forty-three mouths to feed and a Wiebo-imposed virtual ban on store-purchased goods, the simple matter of provisioning fills the women's dimensions of days, rooms, fields. Handwritten notes posted by the front door tabulate the berries harvested and canned so far this season: 126 gallons of saskatoons, fifteen gallons of raspberries, 130 gallons of highbush cranberries, eighty-two gallons of strawberries. "The reward of your labours is to eat," Mamie says, quoting Ecclesiastes.

Everywhere, the farm is devoted to the rewards of eating. Half a dozen lush and tidy vegetable gardens spread over the compound, and the cool, loamy air of the root cellar dug into the hillside bears silent testament. A drying house is filled with racks of hanging herbs and flowers: stinging nettle, chamomile's lacy mist, thyme, golden calendula, all destined for the big-bellied jars that line the kitchen's open shelves.

Later in the afternoon, Wiebo, once again all smiles, shows me a south-facing greenhouse the size of a small bungalow. A massive stone wall bisecting the interior collects and radiates heat, and hinged mirrors hanging from the ceiling reflect light. Five solar chimneys along the windows have reflectors like blind eyes mounted on their surfaces. The windows hum as they swing open and closed without the touch of human hands. The floor is warm, plenum-heated by chimney air circulating below grade. A meticulously crafted stone wall winds the length of the building, providing a base for the soil beds. The young men milled the oval doorframes; Wiebo laid the rocks. The greenhouse is a thing of beauty, light and airy and lovely to the eye. I sit down on the central wall, jealousy hot in my mouth. I want it all for my own, envy them the gorgeous structure itself as well as the richness of the food it houses, the depth of their homegrown pantry. What effort, how many hands, how much time, built such a greenhouse? The idea of its full potential halts my thinking. To put by enough home-grown fare to truly sustain my family, would I have time for any other pursuits?

During the tour Wiebo intersperses biblical references with quotes from Wendell Berry, the American naturalist, philosopher, and poet, as he explains the family's reasons for self-reliance. "The freedom of your convictions means the freedom to raise your own food," he says, paraphrasing no one but himself. To me, it sounds as if sustainability is the means to an end, not an end in itself: in leaving society, the family is striving to attain freedom from societal oppression. He frowns at me from beneath his heavy eyebrows, almost daring me to contradict him. "My long-term vision is to have 150 community residents, well fed and safe." He nudges me. "Your marriage—its end—it shows the truth of societal breakdown. The coming maelstrom of civil unrest. Will you be safe?"

This time, I don't answer.

≈

Mamie picks up the tour in the spacious outdoor summer kitchen with its own stove, wood-burning and immense, which she laughingly calls her "Dogpatch" stove. When Dave would christen our little stretch of Saskatchewan farmland "Dogpatch" several years later, Mamie's endless labours and her summer kitchen would surge into my memory. In the summer kitchen's airy shade, the girls can greens and put up pickles without heating the rest of the house. They eat outside, too, and swings for the little ones fill the yard beside the awnings that stretch over the porch. A long row of bicycles is interrupted by a few small tricycles, some with tykes aboard, pedalling madly across the grass.

Food work is as endless as the gardens. Feeding all those mouths three meals every day, year-round, is no small matter, and I remember my mother telling me how as a child she and Gran fed the threshing crew for the several days they'd be at the farm each summer, the tons of handmade food that went into the men's bellies while they'd brought in the crop.

Although the men help in the gardens and smokehouse, all the drying, canning, preserving, animal husbandry, and cheese-making is the domain of women, as has been the habit around the globe for millennia. At Trickle Creek, four freezers are full and overflowing. Glass jars crammed with dried herbs crowd together on kitchen shelves. Downstairs, more glass jars, these ones filled with high summer produce converted into pickles and relishes, are aligned row by row, destined to brighten winter's pale plates. In the root cellar, where Mamie keeps a big barrel of sauerkraut fermenting during fall and winter, six pork haunches lie, curing prior to being hung in the smokehouse.

Later that afternoon, Mamie's granddaughter Mercy straddles a bicycle, balancing full buckets of milk on the handlebars, and heads for the kitchen from the barn. Behind her in the stable, goats and ewes placidly munch as daughters and granddaughters milk them.

Next day a two-litre stainless steel bucket full of yellow cream as thick as honey stands on the kitchen counter. Several of the younger girls heat milk and add rennet, then cut the resulting curds with big kitchen knives. Finally, an alabaster wheel of goat's milk Gouda emerges from the cheese press. Small hands sprinkle handfuls of gritty salt onto its smooth surface. Then the bulky cheese is lugged downstairs. I follow, and go goggle-eyed when I see dozens of wheels of Gouda, a gleam emanating from shelf after shelf in the dark basement. It's hard to be anything but impressed. Wonder Women, in headscarves and long skirts.

≈

Later, I sit in my room again, the only place for privacy—life at Trickle Creek is collective, as the eldest daughter, Harmony, says: "We have everything in common except wives and underwear."[3] In silence, I contemplate the enormity of what those women and girls produce. Their pride in their accomplishments is tangible, and in truth, there is a lot to envy. I consider myself a throwback in many ways, because I insist on growing and cooking my own food, but this clan of women puts my efforts to shame. Their lives, too, cause jolts of envy: the evidence of family life in an intergenerational enclave. Children on bicycles and babes in arms in the same household as aunts and mothers and grandmothers. Interdependence. The easy assumption of a safety net of their own devising, and a safe place for older, worn-out women to land when their working days are done.

My maternal forebears, the Hutterites, established the same kind of safety net for their elders with colony life, which continues in parts of Western Canada. On Colonies, older women who have held positions of high responsibility, like running the kitchen or communal daycare, retire at a relatively young age. As I age, the attraction of such a safe and respected state grows. The alternative that prevails in our society—the total invisibility and devaluation of any woman past thirty or forty—is not attractive, wise, considerate, or pleasant: I have experienced it already, in the society that Wiebo so despises.

≈

Independence requires power. The farm produces bio-diesel from used cooking oil scavenged from restaurants, and a wind turbine stands on a meagre hill, converting wind to energy for the generator that powers the farm's existence, while twenty solar panels rotate toward the sun.

The increasing isolation of the farm means its inhabitants must master other skills, as well, studying with local specialists. One daughter is learning to become a vet, delivering calves and kids with careful hands. Another is a dental student. Still another is an herbalist, tending a large plot of medicinal herbs the family relies on for healing and for use in soap making: valerian, chamomile, mint, hyssop, comfrey, stinging nettle. Some of the women weave wool from the farm's sheep, dyeing the wool with calendula, marguerite daisies, and onion skins, carding, spinning, felting.

Life on Trickle Creek isn't completely self-sufficient: the farm's building and construction costs are underwritten by the labour of the young men, who work as painters and drywallers throughout the Peace Country. But while Mamie has an "indulgence budget" for things the family can't grow, like rice, vanilla, and coffee, almost everything else edible is produced on-site. Just as my grandparents did, and as I try to do, from my own garden, my CSA connections, my province-wide network of growers. The Ludwig family has been following locavore principles long before the hundred-mile diet emerged as a *cause célèbre*. If some calamity interrupted the normal flow of North American life, I suspect that Trickle Creek Farm would keep trickling along in safety and abundance.

≈

Mamie puts several bottles of her fruit wine into my hands before I depart. "Take this home and lay it down," she urges. It's made from berries and rosehips, dandelions, saskatoons, and highbush cranberries. I would think of Mamie and her busy hands when I plant a pair of cranberry shrubs outside my front door in the fall of 2017.

I drive the long road home. The story is written, filed, the magazine issue appears. My life moves on. But to my utter surprise, when the CBC reports Wiebo's death in April 2012, my life shrinks a little.

His death isn't unexpected: Wiebo called a press conference a year earlier to announce it. He was dying, he said, of esophageal cancer, and he would take no extreme measures to extend his life. He'd spent a lifetime battling Big Oil, and I guessed that he believed his illness had the same cause as his stillborn grandchildren: sour gas emissions from nearby wells.

More than a decade after meeting Wiebo, I am still unwinding the threads of the complexity that attracted and repelled me. Andrew Nikiforuk's obituary for Wiebo in *The Tyee* helps to clarify my mixed feelings about this complicated man. Wiebo "raged against the machine long before it became fashionable . . . [and] will be remembered as a complicated and often angry man who raised unsettling questions about individual rights, corporate power, police methods and government accountability in a petro state." He built his own coffin, Nikiforuk wrote, "with the deliberation of a man who feared nobody except God."[4]

Trickle Creek's inhabitants continue to challenge the incursions of Big Oil into their part of Peace Country. Their population has increased, their babies delivered by Ludwig midwives, and their shared labours keep the farm afloat. Mamie, Jr., completed her informal apprenticeship with a local dentist and has taken on the family's dental care, and a son-in-law serves as the compound's chemist as they move closer to complete off-the-grid status and ending any reliance on conventional fuel.

I understand temper—my sons and I have the same temper my father struggles to master, but these days, my beliefs fall into the Gandhi camp of passive resistance to authority. And I understand—I think—a small part of what drove

Wiebo. For his perseverance, his commitment, his fearless stance, his often-brutal honesty, his willingness to speak his mind, his defence of the natural world, his true reading of the greed of Big Oil, I commend Wiebo Ludwig. But for his bullying, proselytizing, mean streak, misogyny, and his arson: no. It's impossible to not mourn the passing of a passionate soul, even harder to ignore the death of someone who lived by a creed of handmade self-reliance. But as I light a candle for this saboteur, eco-warrior, preacher, misogynist, survivalist, I wonder how many other candles burn in remembrance.

In trying to understand Wiebo, I finally allowed myself to ask my own father questions about his upbringing, questions I might never have had the nerve to ask if I hadn't withstood Trickle Creek. My dad and I have come through the fire; I still love him, and I have forgiven him. Each time I see him, we greet each other with a quick nose-to-nose peck that gives me the chance to see the love that he no longer tries to hide, shining in his brown eyes.

Mostly, I have forgiven myself, as well, for my weaknesses when my marriage was failing, and I pray for my son to find his own peace.

THE PLEASURE
OF YOUR COMPANY

I never anticipated that a life spent feeding others would mean I'd go hungry myself. It's not like I am wasting away, and the house is full of food—the fridge crammed with this season's cherries and last week's leftovers; the freezer overflowing with ducks and other free-range fowl; the counters that hug our kitchen cluttered with tins of spices and jars of tea. Most of what fills our cupboards is homemade. But invitations to dine are thinner than store-bought stock.

No one minds telling me why they don't invite me over. They all say it's intimidating to feed a chef. "I could never invite you to dinner," each of my friends exclaims. "What would I possibly cook for *you*?" What makes it harder to bear is that this exclamation is often delivered at the tail end of a long paragraph filled with loving details describing a glorious meal recently cooked—and served to someone else.

I do have friends who have learned the importance of feeding the cook. Most of them are cooks themselves. Some are not.

Jeff, my previous partner, learned early how important it was to feed me. Not just because I am so much more cheerful (and, more importantly, polite) when I'm well fed, but because he knew that it gave me the sense of feeling cared-for and coddled, exactly what my years of professional cooking provided for others. The downside: when he cooked, we consumed packaged foods, "bag" salads, and invariably, lots of boiled meat and spuds. Motivated entirely by my stomach, I taught him how to braise, so he mastered simply seasoned but succulent short ribs, shanks, and lamb shoulder. Vegetables were another story. Mostly, they got ignored. Raised on The Rock that is Newfoundland, Jeff never met a vegetable he didn't want to overcook or eat from a can. The very first meal he ever cooked for me included broccoli that had cooked for forty-five minutes. Yes, it was appalling. I nibbled, said thanks, and we gently sparred about cooking times for broccoli during our years together, with home field advantage going to whoever was the cook of the day. He moderated his timing somewhat, although he never quit liking his broccoli soft.

What I learned from one mate, I translated to life with another. When my husband, Dave, is in the kitchen, I flop on the couch or perch at the counter with a glass of wine. Without offering advice unless he asks. I continue to say thank you, and I mean it.

Outside my own home, I eat regularly at my friend Sarah-jane's table. My first meal with her was not auspicious. I arrived with my two sons, then preteens, in tow. Sarah-jane shepherded them and her own two sons out to play and poured the wine. Dinner, when it materialized, was modest. To say it was good would be stretching the truth into a pretzel. A jar of Marmite and a plateful of burnt grilled cheese sandwiches appeared on the table, delivered with Sarah-jane's customary slightly caustic, decidedly ironic British wit. We ignored the Marmite, ate the sandwiches, said thank you, meant it. My kids, adventurous diners from year one, took them in stride and enjoyed the crunchy bits. I, too, took them in stride and enjoyed the conversation and ensuing friendship. Sarah-jane is a painter, and a year or two later, the first piece of her art that she gave me was a small pen-and-ink sketch of a burnt grilled cheese sandwich. When we go over to eat I sometimes take over and finish cooking dinner, but not always. Sarah-jane finally got a new stove, a good one. She raved as much about it as I did, but likely for slightly different reasons.

My girlfriend Phyllis and her two daughters, my goddaughters, were the feminine counterpoint to my mostly male household. With them, I sat on the couch, eating macaroni and cheese and drinking red wine, watching endless episodes of *Doctor Who*. The table might have been our laps, but the bond was genuine. They liked to have me there eating with them, and I was equally pleased. It was only macaroni, but I liked it.

Please. Invite me. Make anything. Order in. Pick up sandwiches. Hand me an apron, a knife, a tea towel, and ask me to help, if that makes it any easier. Some of the best meals are collaborative, and I am never shy about mincing carrots or peeling cucumbers in someone else's kitchen, if *that* makes it any easier. I promise that I won't criticize your knives, your chopping style, your pots and pans, or your stove. I *will* say thank you, and mean it. But don't try to impress me with food you don't know and love, and don't attempt overwrought dishes clipped from a foodie file online.

My friend Leona has a wonderful attitude. Once a month during summer, she hosts a First Friday party for her friends, held, as the name suggests, on the first Friday afternoon of the month. At a recent gathering, Leona and her husband, Murray, whipped up some Turkish meze inspired by a recent trip, succulent mouthfuls of snacky things similar to Spanish tapas and

Italian antipasti, some bites laced with pomegranate molasses, others dusted with the lemony nip of sumac. As she handed me a napkin, she reminded me, "You are the guest. Try to enjoy not cooking for once!" It was wise advice. Only a few times have I shown up at her home with a plateful of food or helped with the garlic or the almonds, and then I felt guilty for the garlic scent that clung to my favourite sweater.

Christmas Eve has evolved to include an annual high tea hosted by our friend Honor and her husband, another Dave, in memory of her British aunt. It's not too high, though, and features modest fare we all enjoy—sausages, carrot sticks and celery with English cream dressing, a basket of good bread, a platter of cheeses, and another of sweet tarts. And many kinds of tea by the potful. The point, of course, is conviviality and sharing. The eight of us who gather invariably tell tales at the table, as happens, and we all usually go home with a gift from one or another of the guests—a little steamed pudding and hard sauce, boozy Christmas cake, sometimes homemade sausages and English muffins from Dave and me.

I am not a fussy eater, especially when I don't have to cook it myself. Well, that is not quite true. I am a particular eater, but I have learned that there is a time for choosiness, and it never occurs when my knees are tucked under someone else's home table. Trust me, my mom taught me to be a very good guest. I say please, and thank you (many times), and I will even clear the table after dinner. And show me the dishwasher; I am all over loading it. It is the least I can do.

For some unwilling hosts, the issue is exacerbated because I not only cook, but I have written, too, about cooks and cooking. Maybe they have me confused with the razor-witted, sharp-penned editor or reviewer who slashes and burns with red blood instead of ink. Look, just because I can spell *zabaglione* as well as make it doesn't mean I expect you to! (Although it really is easy. You start with a few eggs and sugar, some elbow grease, Marsala, and a whisk, a potful of simmering water, a bowl . . .) But I suspect that to some, creating food on the printed page is as weighty as the apple tart or the shepherd's pie that I yearn to tuck into at my friends' tables. Honest, all I want is a chance to sit at your table and share. I just want the pleasure of your company, and food cooked by other hands.

Modest food is fine. In fact, it is preferred. You don't really think that chefs and food writers eat fancy stuff every day at home, do you? The truth is that most chefs who make their living with "fancy-panties" frou-frou food prefer to eat plain and simple stuff on their own time. It's a little odd, that gulf between what suits a chef's professional pride and what suits her personal palate. This particular cook is partial to crispy-skinned roasted chicken gilded with olive oil and herbs, half an onion and a twist of thyme stuck in its gullet, or bowls filled with hearty helpings—curried lamb, lentils and rice, leek and potato soup, scrambled eggs and buttery toast. Or mashed potatoes and anything slowly braised. Or anything flavoured with bits of double-smoked bacon. See? Lots of choices! Nothin' fancy, as my grandmother Sarah used to say when we sat down at her old kitchen table. It wasn't fancy, but it was real, substantial fare, set out on the table with the casualness of daily love.

The reality that I have absorbed into my bones and my being, assimilated like the aroma of chicken stock infiltrating the kitchen walls, is the importance of the meal shared. Cooks are the biblical Marthas, as Margaret Atwood named them in *The Handmaid's Tale*, the ones standing behind the loaded table, anxious to ensure that all is served, all are happy, all is well. We have learned that eating together is an everyday event, but not one to be taken lightly. It is chief among the small recurrent moments, the everyday and the ordinary, that define our lives and who we are.

PRODIGAL

A church, miles from town, interjects peeling white paint into the clouds. A sagging wire gate stands open above a faded sign, vowels missing like teeth from a tired mouth: COMMUN TY SUMM R SUPP R TH S SUND Y. ALL WELC ME!

The minister waits at the door, several men beside him, ball caps in hands. A band of white skin, innocent as a child's, stripes the forehead of each weathered face just above the eyebrows. The men fiddle with their caps, shift their work boots on the wooden stairs, avoid looking at me.

Ron Thiessen's tenor voice is mild. "The congregation's waiting," he calls. "Chicken, ham, and potato salad. And pie. Just a brief service first."

"I'll just be a minute," I say. Dave and I turn to the cemetery, where my youngest brother and my grandparents lie under leathery tufts of sage. It's been years since I walked this path, and I have forgotten where their graves are.

After five minutes, we give up the search and climb the stairs. Ron has left the door open, and the hinges squeal as we pull it closed. He is standing behind the pulpit. Waiting. Faces turn to stare at us as we enter, the door scraping on the sill behind us. The narrow stairs squeak as we climb to the balcony and slide into two spots in the last pew. The afternoon light pours through high windows set with modest rectangles of stained glass, emphasizing the cracked drywall and rough floors. We stand and sit, and stand and sit again, sing hymns I thought I'd forgotten, their words coming automatically into my mouth. Amazing grace. Blessed be. Rugged cross. Peace. Sisters brothers. Beside me, Dave's voice is muffled, slightly off-key.

After the blessing, we make our way downstairs and into the kitchen, where long tables are edged with folding chairs. More closed faces examine us; only the minister greets us as we join the queue at the buffet table heaped with sliced ham and colourful jellied salads. Behind the shuttered faces of the congregation, I imagine questions that will be asked behind our backs, later, at home. "Who's he? *She* has the look of Sarah, maybe, or old Suzie." But no one introduces themselves, or takes our hands.

After supper, the minister falls in step with us as we resume the search for my brother's gravestone. "Glenn was my close friend through our teenage years," he reminds me, "through all those years of school. God has him safe now." I know he is referring to the motorcycle accident that ended Glenn's life at nineteen: Ron was with him, and identified his body for the police.

We stop and stoop to read eroding gravestones, dates and names vanishing under the ruthless prairie wind. On some, all that remains is the anonymity of settled sand and accruing dust. Finally I find Glenn's grave, the metal hi-hat from his drum kit my dad had embedded in the stone surface the most visible clue. In the adjacent row, I locate my grandfather's grave, my Gran's beside him. I call to Dave with relief, "Here they are!"

≈

Dave and I moved to the little sand hills west of Saskatoon in 2010, after endless deliberation about the possibility of rural life far from Calgary, where I raised my two sons. As part of a gypsy air force brood, I'd spent my childhood as a visitor, observing other, more settled families from the outside. I belonged nowhere. For my own boys, I chose the slow rust of stability: one city, one school.

While my boys grew up, I navigated Albertan range roads, visiting gardeners and farmers, imagining their dwellings as my own. I tried on country homes the way other women try on shoes. Standing in the kitchen of a white clapboard farmhouse on the central plateau, or in a veranda-wrapped ranch bungalow in the foothills, I wondered, *Is this home? Do I fit here?*

≈

Dad was a lost soul with a houseful of preteen kids when he left the air force, disillusioned by the fall of the Avro Arrow and the inevitable end of his aviation career. We were teenagers when he yielded gracelessly to Grampa's suggestion of one last move.

"I'm no farmer," my southern Ontarian father said pointedly.

"You will be," my mother replied. Nearly twenty years had passed since she'd flown the chicken coops and fields at eighteen, unwilling to be a farm wife. But she fit, the hand returning to the glove, and within ten years of our move, Dad was debating weather and the Wheat Board as vehemently as his neighbours, the wind rasping off his hard edges.

My older sister stayed in the Fraser Valley. My teenaged brothers shrugged and made friends among our shirttail prairie cousins, but I stubbornly disdained life under the big sky, and like Mom, I flew away as soon as I completed high school three years later. Then two of my brothers left on their own ebb tides. Only Glenn, the youngest, remained. Of all of us, he was most like Grampa. Bulky and laconic, they shared a crooked grin and a fondness for sly puns and kites. On my holiday visits home, I watched Glenn's hands untangle bridle and line, then from the field south of the yard effortlessly cast the year's new kite into the sky, where it hung on the wind in profound silence. Without ever discussing it, we all considered Glenn the natural candidate to next occupy the farmhouse. Then the unexpected silenced our assumptions: Glenn's death at nineteen.

≈

At seventy, Mom developed a limp and Dad started to stoop. His back rebelled at the mention of hours on a tractor, and during a spring phone conversation in 2008, my mother reluctantly admitted, "Stop sending gardening gizmos. Between my bad knees and his back, we're not putting in another garden." After a little prodding, she told us, her four surviving children, "Your father wants to move to town."

The rest remained unsaid, but the words hung in the air like my brother's kite: *do you want to take on the farm?*

My brothers and sister promptly and loudly said no.

It took me two years to say yes. My parents correctly anticipated my eventual response, that I'd only want the house and yard, not the farm. They sold off the land surrounding the home quarter, including the quarter section containing the original access driveway to the north. My father engineered a new driveway west from the yard.

I'm no farmer either. I come home to write. Dave is an established poet and fiction writer, and I have my eyes fixed on sharing the literary world he inhabits. My hectic life in Calgary has become a frustrating one, with little time or energy left over for literature. The peace and solitude I envision at the farm finally make sense.

Dave, a long-time Regina resident, spent a year as Saskatoon library's writer-in-residence. He has friends in the city from that time, and they, along with other writers I've met at artists' and writers' colonies, enthusiastically agree to help us paint the house before we move in.

I drive the six hours from Calgary with my eldest son, Darl, a cooler jammed with food, my rollers, and paint brushes. Dave drives his truck north from Regina, the truck's box crammed with bike, furniture, books. Neighbours offer us a bed during the cleanup project, and we spend an evening studying the land's familiar geography before we begin.

≈

The house began in 1910. Mom claims it was a cursory affair of two grain bins bolted together and a basement dug out beneath them. A long kitchen with a roof angled like a jaunty fedora brim was slung along the west side. The room on the north side, my grandparents' perpetually cool and dark bedroom, became my refuge during childhood summer visits. When my family arrived in 1973, it morphed into my brothers' bedroom, and a year later, when running water was finally piped into the house, it changed again, into a bathroom. Dad added a basement bedroom for me, then two east-facing bedrooms with an expansive studio loft above them. Ten years later, he built a glassed-in sunroom adjacent to the kitchen. Dave and I will learn to love the sunroom's spacious brightness, and it will become our reading room, dining room, and Dave's office, but on this June evening as we await the start of our painting foray, I register only the twenty windows with wide sills that make up three sides of the room, and foot after foot of moulding. "This room will take months to paint," I groan to Darl.

Our friends swarm out from Saskatoon, some calling after getting lost en route on the gravel grid of country roads: "We're somewhere, where are you?"

Eventually we have a buzzing hive, four or five people in each room, stroking on trim, painting walls, taping windows. My tall son Darl works ahead of us, rolling white onto each ceiling in his first-ever painting foray; then he washes the paint from his hair and hands, and together we grill sausages and burgers. The two-day painting bee converts the house to bumblebee yellow. I belatedly, gratefully, recall that the kitchen had been yellow in my grandparents' day. The tide of warmth and welcome hangs in the farmhouse, enveloping me in the warmest aspects of prairie residence and making me part of a community.

The next morning, I leave our neighbours' house and walk the driveway in the early-morning coolness, and sit on the kitchen floor, watching light arc through the windows. The yellow walls carry me back to my grandmother's day—tall slatted cupboards, butter-toned, the cookie tin out of reach, the wood stove's water reservoir warm against my back. My grandmother's rough hands, square like mine, the translucent, tensile skin of strudel dough separating our palms.

≈

I quickly learn that rural living is like life on the beach, without the holiday. Sand is inescapable. Dogs come and go, depositing mud on each trip. The wind rarely rests. Window ledges and floors are always gritty, reminders of the prairie waiting to reclaim its stake.

The yard and nearby Gopher Hill—named for the rodents who carved its geography into a bustling subterranean settlement—are crowded with abandoned cars and trucks and ancient farm implements, grass growing through their gill-like radiators, legacy of three generations of tinkering men mindful of what might be needed on another day. The pump, ensconced in its own building across the yard, draws water from the original sixty-five-foot well. Before running water was installed— several years after my family's arrival in 1973—the backyard privy was a mid-winter dash, and water was toted indoors in white enamel buckets from the pumphouse, the water's hard minerals slowly thinning the metal pails into red membranes.

≈

Most rural houses perch on the lip of the road, but ours, built when the barn was a "stopping place" for settlers traversing the Battleford Trail on foot with oxen and horses pulling Red River carts, is half a kilometre in from the gravel roads to the north and west. Our acreage sits in the cup of the local watershed, a subtle decline of ten feet.

In spring 2011, while still saturated from the previous year's unseasonably wet summer, the province melts, then floods, in what is dubbed the flood event of the century. Our lower elevation and our long driveway are suddenly— shockingly—relevant.

Water pools over the driveway, glitters on fields and yard. Fifteen of our eighteen acres and many acres of adjacent land are transformed into lake. The shore, lapping forty feet from our house, is soon edged with duckweed and cattails, filled with black snails and frogs. How long have their embryos slept before waking? Water demands entry to the outbuildings, sleeps four feet deep in the hay barn, takes up residence in the stand of aspens.

We live in a postcard, its frame closed. The ATV is our only way in and out. "Do we *really* need to go to town?" becomes our mantra, and dismay colours our regard for coat hooks laden with rain gear, mosquito gear, mud gear.

We trade in our low-slung city cars, including my beloved yellow Beetle, for a Jeep, and are able to drive to our door when the old north driveway emerges from the muck, the track my brothers and I had hiked to catch the school bus, a route now on land my family no longer owns. Riding a neighbour's ATV on someone else's land, uncertainty triggers longing for my sons, both still in Calgary, aches that press-gang me and interrogate my decision to live here.

It seemed a clear-cut choice in fast-paced Calgary. As a freelance culinary writer and educator, my existence was chancy and physically demanding: I came home exhausted from teaching evening classes. The next day, I'd be too pooped to write, my joy in food diminished. Something had to change. I wanted time to write literature, the poems and stories pecking away in my brain. A rural life seemed like an ideal solution. The reality—a quirky old house thirty kilometres from town, compounded by a flood—is less idyllic.

≈

Water attracts waterfowl. Gazing through the expanding iris of Dad's telescope, we learn to identify horned grebes in gold masks like Mardi Gras celebrants, ruddy ducks by their blue bills, coots by their imitations of poorly tuned Evinrudes. In May, the courting frogs create a thrumming wall of sound, and in July, the blue and amber dragonflies arrive to voraciously consume the mosquitoes that attend waterfront living.

So many mosquitoes. Each morning, heading along the lakeside to the barn to feed the inherited cats and count the kittens, I windmill my arms to clear a path through swarms of insects. We consume granola and coffee outdoors on the deck, hummingbirds darting past us to the feeder, until the mosquitoes find us. Most evenings, we retreat indoors. I start to feel resentful, wear impervious raingear while I'm outdoors, buy every mosquito-repelling candle and torch I can find, build an esplanade of flame and citronella around our picnic table. "It would be funny if I didn't itch so much," I tell Dave, scratching irritably at a new bite on my ankle.

The real irony is contained in the weekly trips to town to buy drinking water. Our well has been contaminated by the E. coli in the water that surrounds us, memento of cattle grazing the area in bygone decades. We commission a new well, but even so, the new well still draws up water that is high in iron and mineral content. The water is sound but it leaves calcified scale on all our appliances. I put buckets under the eaves to collect rainwater for the houseplants, water that our dogs and cats prefer to the tap water we fill their bowls with.

In my second-storey studio, the sound of water seeps into my stories and poems, as unpredictable as any character. I gaze for hours at the south field where teals dabble past my high-water mark, a rusty Model A, its chassis drowned.

Our neighbours graze cattle in the field beyond our lake, and we consign some of their beef to our freezer. For my birthday, Dave buys me a smoker; I brine and smoke a brisket and give him pastrami on homemade sourdough. I pack our pantry with home-cured bacon, smoked sausages, asparagus pickles. Every tomato seed germinates, a riot of heirloom colours, and lunch is a hit parade of BLTs and just-snipped arugula.

≈

My grandmother and my mother hoed spuds where my garden absorbed sunlight in our first year. "Granddad grazed cattle here. There's a bed of manure *this* deep," Mom said soon after we arrived, straddling the asparagus patch, gesturing with her cane. "Good thing it's not a dry year," she added wryly as I steered the garden tractor around rows as tightly spaced as molars, a misplaced habit with roots in my previous pocket-sized urban garden. The entire perennial garden—asparagus, black currants, strawberries, raspberries, rhubarb—would drown before the next spring.

Microclimate. Geology. Humility. Hanging in the hall is a photo from my grandparents' time, the house and yard surrounded by well-tended windrows of caragana and tidy pastures. I cringe as I plough through thigh-high weeds to my studio to write, glad my granddad is not here to witness my slack ways as a steward of the land.

"Use Roundup," Dad suggests as I rip white veins of encroaching quack grass out of the soil. The fact that I even consider taking his suggestion seriously, after years of writing about chemical-free sustainable growing, is a red flag I cannot ignore, sparking dinner debates for weeks. Can an aging gardener maintain an organic footprint? Can I cultivate a no-fly zone, mulch, continue to hand-pull roots? Or do I acknowledge the power of the teeming, wild landscape we balance so precariously beside, nature at her most insistent, anxious to take back the garden? My admiration for my mother, who maintained the garden single-handedly for over thirty years, skyrockets.

Beets, the season's final harvest, taste like our soil, earthy, mineral-rich. Most days, I count the costs we've paid to live on this land as worthwhile. I have become a full-time writer. I miss my sons, my friends, but not city life. The sound of coyote song, the beauty of the lake and its inhabitants, the peace of rural life, the trusting faces of kittens greeting me each morning, all feel like sufficient reasons to stay.

≈

In November, the flooded land freezes. Birds leave in small flocks, diminishing circles in a shrinking pond, two dozen, one dozen, a handful of coots. One day, I toss an inscribed stone onto the ice. It rattles and rings, unexpectedly loud reverberations, until it hits a protruding fencepost. Beyond it, a transient goose watches, curious. Nature isn't done with us yet. Our drowned driveway becomes an ice road, but neither Dave nor I have the nerve to drive our Jeep along its wide shoulders.

December arrives, and with it, bitter cold. We have learned to insert compressed air into the water pump, and how to re-prime it, and to buff corrosion from the electrical contacts, but each time we retreat to the house for restorative beverages afterward. The fragility of our lifeline is unnerving, and constant anxiety about the pump dogs us both. Then it slows to a crawl. One morning, Dave opens the tap to air gurgling through empty pipes. We bundle into parkas, gloves, toques, boots, and trek into the west wind's teeth, across the yard to the pumphouse. It's easy to imagine, as snow swirls around us, how simple it would have been in the settlers' time to lose the way and wander into the white, just a few hundred yards from safety and warmth.

The pumphouse is silent, the well stilled. Dave and I stare helplessly at each other. We aren't handy enough to jerry-rig a solution; we don't even understand the problem. I think, for the umpteenth time, that the wrong sibling took on this place. Either of my brothers, good with cars, machinery, hand tools, might have avoided this dilemma, and either could solve it without calling city plumbers who charge mileage to visit acreages. I'm too disappointed to cry.

Four days crawl by before a technician arrives with a new pump. When his task is completed, I will feel a weight of worry lift free and disappear, but during the delay, I stoically melt snow to use in the toilet and to water the plants. While we wait, without water flowing though the lines, the septic tank freezes, and sewage begins to back up into our already damp basement.

We pry the heavy circular lid off the septic tank, lower a pair of heaters strung on wire hangers like mobiles, and heap pink insulation over the recovered concrete. I rummage an old quilt out of the truck, marvelling at how things morph into unexpected usefulness, and we tuck it around the lid, anchoring it with bricks we pry up from the walkway. When we retire to the kitchen and the reassuring sound of running water, our restorative pot of tea tastes bitter despite the honey I stir in. All I need to know arrives after I need it, and learning is wearing me down.

≈

To ring in the New Year, we make proverbial lemonade. I mix red food colouring with water, and we paint concentric rings on the ice. We fill vinegar jugs, leave them outdoors to freeze, and invite our friends to a jam-pot bonspiel. The day is bright and mild. I don my Black Watch kilt over three pairs of tights, a Fair Isle wool sweater, and Darl's old fleece jester's hat, then light a fire at the edge of the lake to heat the cider. Dozens of people come to curl, bringing kids and skates. The old threshing machine and auger look like time-warped dinosaurs frozen in the Cretaceous, waiting for the ancient beach to rise again. The day spent laughing cleanses me.

The day after New Year's, I go to the church, three miles away, to talk to my dead brother and grandparents.

"Everything is two-sided," I tell their gravestones. "Is it always like that?"

I know better than to expect an answer in straightforward language. At the edge of the cemetery, deer tracks punctuate the snow. I leave my own imprint, fluttered wings and home-bound boots of a prairie snow angel, and wonder if it will be visible tomorrow. When I get home at dusk, coyote song surrounds me, echoing from the vast and silent landscape. Living under the swathe of Saskatchewan stars feels like home, for all its failings. That simple fact still surprises me.

HANDMADE

When my sons were small, I often took them to the fabric store. Dailyn, my youngest, would run his fingers over waterfalls of satin, velvet like ripe peaches, the slubby resistance of silk, assessing texture and drape with the touch of a born connoisseur. As a five-year-old, his colour preferences leaned to bright yellows smeared like broken eggs over charcoal, but even then he knew instinctively that knowledge resides in the hands. Back at home, I pinned, cut, then sat down at my Elna and whirred pieces of cloth into archers' tunics, wizards' robes resplendent with comets and starbursts, jazzy tasselled two-toned jesters' hats. We played made-up games in made-up countries, with made-up characters, each attired in their own costume.

Both boys gravitated toward my chefs' whites as they hung in my closet after laundering, smelling of fresh air instead of garlic or onions. They would wrap the mark of my trade around themselves, lost in the folds of material, plucking at the knotted cloth buttons marching down the jacket-front as they paraded down the hallway to the kitchen. It wasn't that my whites and what they represented were mysterious, or foreign territory to them. Far from it. My sons were already intimately acquainted with the landscape of food, and my whites were the most comfortable and comforting clothing they knew.

≈

Dailyn, visiting from Calgary, finds me in the kitchen of the old Saskatchewan farmhouse I now live in. He takes the bowl of bread dough from my hands, plops it on the counter, yards off his sweater to reveal a baker's biceps. "Here, let me," he says, dusting his hands with flour. He kneads effortlessly, hands working in a double-time crossover-rhythm that is smooth and effective, rapid, unhurried.

"It's a braided Finnish bread called *pulla*," I tell him. "Five strands, like challah."

"Show me the braiding sequence. I don't know how." So I roll ropes of dough, fold the ends, interweave the strands, chanting the sequence like a mantra: two over three, five over two, one over three. After I finish the first loaf, he steps in. "It looks a bit rough, Mom."

"Been awhile."

"Yeah? It shows." As he rolls and shapes them, the ropes are well-behaved, mooring themselves one to the next without twists or tangles, as guy lines heed a skilled deckhand. Within minutes, he's made seven loaves, each snug and matter-of-factly tidy, waiting to bloom in the oven under a tempera-like glaze of egg yolk and cream. His hands on the dough are sturdy, not as delicate or as long as his brother's piano-playing fingers, but workman-like, an artisan's hands, fine-tuned through the generations for doing, making, gauging, assessing. When he catches me studying him, he winks and flexes his left arm. "I make bazillions of buns and loaves every morning at work," he says with unabashed pride. An hour later, when the loaves emerge from the oven, he pulls apart the intricacy of the crusted braid with fingers as facile as a jeweller's, sniffing delicately —a rabbit assessing a carrot crop before tasting. "That's cardamom I can smell under all that butter, right?" Between us, we consume half a loaf while it is still warm.

If flour is of earth, and water is water, then yeast is of air—that which elevates. Fire is the element of transformation, what magicks the other three. Cooks know this, are drawn to gas ranges, wood stoves, open-flame barbecue pits, beachside grills, anywhere fire is visible. That transformation—the heating blast of the sun and its hint of the beyond—turns raw ingredients into dinner, untutored children into young men and women, citizens of clay into golden heroes. Fire is the cook's first and best tool. Life is the crucible.

Both my sons outgrew my whites years ago. For a while they wear their own each day, both in the same restaurant, one the baker, the other a line cook. I visit them at work, sit at the counter on the guests' side, my boys a world away from me in the open kitchen that is the restaurant's nerve centre. Darl, his face covered with shining beads, is at the wood-fired rotisserie, its heat drawing sweat from me ten feet away. He sets down my plate, crosses his arms, leaning against his side of the counter, studying my reaction as I slice through the hashmarks of grilled scallops perched on a quarter-head of grilled romaine dressed in olive oil, capers, and lemon zest. "Good, eh?" I nod, my mouth full. Dailyn delivers molten chocolate tart and ice cream and cookie and coulis, elements arranged on the white plate like art, then hangs around, grinning, as I match up textures, bite by bite.

Cooking is an intensely physical profession, drastically underpaid for the stamina, skills, and contribution it demands and offers. I don't expect either of them to make it their life's work and have encouraged them to have a plan, a skill beyond the stove so they can exit the kitchen before they hit thirty-six, as I did. Their adult years in commercial kitchens have already wrought changes in them, changes that began inside and manifested outwardly, as bulging biceps and muscular hands, as tough skin that seems impervious to hot pans, as the grace of dancers pivoting at the stove, as calmness when pots boil over and flames gutter out and deadlines measure success in seconds.

Over and over again, I remind myself that they are independent beings, young men responsible for their own growth and well-being. It's difficult to remember, though, whenever they call in an upset, their voices raised or strained, to rant about the long hours and poor pay of their chosen jobs. Electricians, carpenters, and plumbers earn double or triple a well-paid line cook's hourly wage, without the exposure to hot ovens, deep fryers filled with searing oil, seven-hundred degree rotisseries. I struggle to remember then that my sons chose paths that fit their ethos, that paths take turns, labyrinthine at times, without obvious end points, the maze's centre invisible during day-to-day living.

We—my sons and siblings and I—are descended from off-colony Hutterites, peasant pacifists renowned in central Europe not just as farmers, but also as artisans. One of my brothers makes wooden furniture, the other is a metal sculptor; my sister spent years at a potter's wheel, throwing clay into useful and gorgeous shapes. My hands, formed from the same mould, have the shape and look of my grandmother's, and of my youngest son's. It's a gift you are born with, to have the hands of a maker, to be grounded in the natural world, to take primal elements and shape them, transform them, and in the doing, serve as focal point and translator for those at a remove from the natural world. It's not independence—although when I see my sons standing tall in front of the stove, their self-reliance glows around them like an aura—it's interdependence. In cooking, we express our deepest feelings about the nature of the universe, our deepest faith and connection to all that is primal and irresistible. In cooking, we express our choices—our link with nature, our self-reliance, our willingness and ability to care for others—and to manifest the humility and generosity we were born into. But cooking for a living isn't the only way to experience any of those realities.

≈

Darl was seven, Dailyn three, when my husband and I bought a restaurant. Thirty-seven seats, a split level with a pair of elaborately carved carousel ponies mounted on the spindle railing of the divider. Fading hardwood floors, pressed-back chairs, Key Largo fans, and floor-to-ceiling windows—a joint Lauren Bacall would have been comfortable in. A small four-burner Wolf range sat at the heart of the cramped kitchen, a convection oven hemming in its heat on one side, stainless-steel dishwasher humming on the other, with just enough space for one person to stand in front of the Wolf. After school that fall, the boys sat on stools at the narrow counter, watching me work, Darl's long legs swinging, Dailyn's stubby calves folded like a nesting bird's. I gave Darl an apple and a short-bladed serrated knife with a rounded tip. "Peel this," I said, and went back to rolling out my pastry.

"What kind of apple is it?" Darl asked, his fair eyebrows climbing as a long comma of peel dangled floor-ward from his fingers. "Can I eat the peel? Is it a Gala or a Newton or a Granny Smith or a Mac?"

"Of course eat the peel! Taste it, and tell me."

He rescued the ribbon of peel, scrunched his face. "Gala," he answered through the crunching. "It tastes like a Gala." He handed his brother a slice. "Try it, Dailyn."

The next summer, during cherry season, I gave them cherries like tiny fairy globes, some golden, some ruby, others so dark a purple they were almost black. In peach season, they ate peaches, clingstone, freestone, juices like melted amber dribbling down their chins. They watched me whisk vinaigrettes, taste sauces, plate salads, and simmer short ribs, build mousses and meringues; then they rummaged in the shelves of the dry stores in the basement prep kitchen, searching for snacks, ate again and again, went home to their own suppers with our nanny. I read notes from them when I stumbled home late at night, exhausted, reeking of garlic and caramel and roasted meats and coffee. *Mama, we miss you, come cook at home.* I didn't have the words to explain the compulsion that drove me to feed others instead of them, couldn't even explain it to myself. In photographs from that era, my face is haunted, gaunt, my bones almost showing through, my flesh consumed by the fire that fed on my ambition. The compulsion burnt its way throughout my body, and a couple years later, we sold the restaurant. I staggered through the few years as a neophyte food writer in a daze, wondering who I was if I wasn't a chef.

≈

One day Dailyn jumps ship and becomes a waiter at a new resto. "I don't like being taken advantage of," he tells me on the

phone, and details a squabble that has sent him to the Labour
Relations Board to complain about his former boss's overtime
practices. The suit takes months to resolve in Dailyn's favour.
In the coming years, he would spend his off-hours running up
and down mountains in the Rockies and contemplating what
path to take next.

~

Darl's face is tense, his eyes shadowed, when he arrives on my
snowbound farm six hundred kilometres from his apartment.
I'm surprised to see him; he and his brother have moved on to
working six days a week at a hot new resto in Calgary, a place
so jumping that time off is non-existent.

"I quit my job," he says over coffee and a plateful of muffins.
"I found myself crying in the dish pit. Couldn't eat. Worrying
about work before I went in. I just can't cook at that stress level." He looks at me, knows I'll understand. "I care too much
about food to cook for a living anymore, Mom. I want to make
things with my hands, but I don't know what." I understand his
conundrum, but don't know either, no matter how badly I'd
love to have an answer for my boy.

A week later, the muscles that line his face are beginning
to relax. He stays up late, communing with the far-off northern lights as they lean closer to the earth to hear the coyotes
carolling. Like the cats perched on the heat register and rocker
in front of the fire, he sleeps in. When he surfaces, I hand him
a mug, remembering the years it took me to find myself, the
artist separate from the cook. We make supper together. As
he dismembers a chicken for the pot, slices an onion, slivers
garlic cloves into shards, I am relieved, watching his sure hands
wielding my knives. It isn't cooking that has damaged him, but
the trade of cooking. In both my boys, their love of making is

intact. It may take years for them to find the answer, but life is the trip, not the arrival. The path has turned beneath their feet and will carry them closer to the heart of the maze, to the men they are meant to become.

ASHES

I'm shovelling ashes from the wood stove into the coal-scuttle when the phone rings: "My cousin has sighted a big white dog. Maybe it's him." But our friend's description doesn't include a black and tan face or floppy two-tone ears, and my hope deflates. Outside, the winter wind catches, a thin coating of grey ash settling along the January snow.

It's been six months and dozens of phone calls since our dog, Mister B, disappeared. With each call, hope restrings itself. Each disappointment leaves me disconnected, aflap in a gale of loss, other losses blowing back into my face and eyes before drifting away. The decades-ago end of my first marriage. My youngest brother's early death. Lovers I've left behind. My grandparents' funerals. My former mother-in-law's slide into dementia. Her death. The ends of my sons' innocence. My own unfulfilled aspirations as a chef. And looming losses in the future that I don't want to name. Grief opens every window.

≈

Mister B watched the summer previously while I dug a new garden bed for half a dozen raspberry canes, angled to face the prairie sun. Once the quack grass was decapitated, its stringy roots excavated, I dug out the heavy clay, then shovelled in peat moss, compost, soil. I was sweat-drenched when I finally tapped on the sunroom's window. Mister B crowded at my elbow, unwilling to miss anything.

"It's time," I shouted, and Dave carried out the urns containing the remains of our two previous dogs. Amigo, a golden-maned lion, had become as unpredictable as any emperor as he aged, scoring my gloves with his clicking teeth whenever he felt threatened. Mojo, a miniature schnauzer who thought he was big, bounced after cats and mice on his self-appointed rounds. I'd crouched beside each dog as he died, smoothing fur, praising the wild world that waited. That August afternoon, after scattering their ashes over the new raspberry patch, we stood at the head of the bed. Neither of us spoke. We mourned, but the way we mourn friends who have lived full and wonderful lives.

≈

Mister B was a Great Pyrenees, a guardian without a flock to guard, so he went visiting as usual on a sunny October Saturday morning after our walk. He was an independent thinker, as dogs bred to guard sheep must be, good at sitting for cookies, not so good at returning when called. I loved him unabashedly—his enthusiasm for soccer, for popcorn, for carolling when coyotes sang, for his beautiful coat, brindled in the shape of a saddle that always made me imagine a wee monkey in a red circus suit as his reckless rider. I'd accepted that I loved him more than he loved me: as a guardian dog, his allegiances lay with other animals, and although he'd been a boisterous and affectionate puppy, he was simply not demonstrative once he became an adult, only rarely leaning on my knee to have his ears rubbed. On our morning walks, he loved to hurdle the bulrushes and cattails that lined the driveway. He wasn't chatty, and only let loose his chesty baritone at night as he stood guard.

I spent that October morning at my desk. When Mister B didn't come home, I scoured our land for a sign of him. After dinner, I walked out the driveway and stared down the sand road, a rural road that is home to eight families on its three-kilometre stretch. Nothing. Next day, I drove onto every yard and asked about Mister B.

Two days passed. I drove our neighbour's ATV through the rain, checking every field. Nothing. I screamed at the indifferent sky, "My dog hates the rain! Hates getting his coat wet! Send him home!"

When I returned the ATV, Ken said, "There's scuttlebutt goin' around."

"What scuttlebutt?"

"I heard two rifle shots Saturday morning. Al mighta been pissed by Mister B barking at his cattle." Al and his wife June lived around the corner from Ken and Sharon.

"Is someone saying Al shot my dog?"

"Not in so many words," Ken said quickly.

But June had denied seeing Mister B when I'd stopped by. "Poppy would run any dog off the yard," she'd said, pointing at the muscular Rottweiler beside her, legs splayed, teeth bared. I'd been afraid to ask further, unwilling to breathe my imagination into reality, unwilling to confront her husband and his dog. Accusing a family of killing your dog without proof is a guarantee of more than enmity.

Next day, Sharon and I slipped through the barbed wire into the pasture, well out of Poppy's range. We spent hours crisscrossing the scrubby sand hills, hoping and not hoping to find Mister B's dog-tags or collar. We found nothing. But it was never likely we would; farmers have front-end loaders on their tractors, and unwanted evidence is easily disposed of in back fields.

In the days and weeks that followed, we posted reward notices, talked to everyone within a five-mile radius, called vets, shelters, radios, internet pet helplines. I blamed myself for Mister B's loss. When we'd acquired him as a pup, fencing the yard had seemed prohibitively expensive, so we'd debated building a dog run, but rationalized that a Great Pyrenees would hate being confined and ultimately let him run free. After all, we told each other, hadn't Amigo and his predecessors had the run of my parents' farm?

But we live in different times. My grandparents' farm had included four contiguous quarter-sections, enough land for even a dog bred in the Spanish highlands as a solitary shepherd. But the land has been chipped away, the quarters halved and sold by my parents. A dozen houses now stand in sight of our yard, too crowded for a big dog to run loose, and the municipality's bylaws prohibit it in any case. In this neighbourhood, there are still people with guns who view shooting a trespassing dog as a right.

≈

A year passes. Every part of my day is haunted by Mister B's absence. I've given up popcorn, which he loved, and some days I hate living here, where my dog is no longer. Every time I drive onto the yard, I pray to see him lying in front of the barn.

Open the gates, therapists and self-help writers advise, to fully experience your inner life, to achieve the deepest experiences. But the wide-open world of faltering maybes, the wild possibility of a sighting, followed by gut-wrenching adrenalin and the inevitable crash—it's exhausting.

Some friends say, "Get on with life and get another dog." They don't mean to be callous. But grief keeps long office hours, and Mister B was a beloved member of our family. There's no replacing his blithe spirit.

The animals in our neighbourhood take notice of his absence. Ken's cattle dumbly watch my solo morning walks. Sharon's donkeys bray when I pass. The deer and coyotes stroll within metres of our house.

I want my dog back. Dave's theory is that Mister B was stolen, a gentler image than the alternatives. I'd rather he was intact, safe, locked behind a high fence so he couldn't return to us. But he weighed 130 pounds, and he hated cars. It would have taken exceptional strength to get him into a car or truck, and I haven't believed in happy endings for decades.

I'd gladly give up tenuous hope for certainty. But there is no riposte to death, no clever comeback, no resurrection through sharp-witted words. There's no shortcut to the experience of bereavement. Only—eventually—acceptance. I fear freezing in this state—what if I wait eternally for what will never return?

Little is worse than unresolved loss. It deflates the soul and leaves behind ashes of emptiness. In ways I only barely understand, I have changed. Crowded on top of my guilt about being afraid to confront Poppy's owner is my bleak assumption of Mister B's violent death. I've always thought myself an optimist, but because he is gone without reason, my faith—in myself, and in the innate goodness of the world—has tarnished. What has been exposed as bedrock is randomness, what we simply cannot comprehend. And unprovable, as issues of philosophy often are, our inhumanity has been revealed, our unthinking cruelty.

≈

This morning after my walk, more than a year after Mister B's disappearance, I shovel the latest ashes from the wood stove and carry the scuttle out to the yard. No dog tags at my heels. An early snowstorm has glazed the path with ice. The last leaves shiver on the white birch. When the ashes settle at my feet in a heap instead of dispersing, I scuff them with my boot as Mister B would have done with his paws. But Mister B's pawprints are gone, and the ashes simply blow away when the breeze picks up.

RAPTURE
~ *for the 25,000*

I first knew rapture in the Methodists' evangelical tent, when my spirit called me to kneel. The feeling of grace was new, luminosity spreading like a favourite quilt. The glow held for a few days, then started to fade and chip, pecked away by the raven's bill of my mother's cynicism. "Saved, eh?" she'd say, then hand me the tea towel, the barn shovel, the floor mop.

Three decades later, rapture again—in an orchard when I rose at daybreak with the migrant pickers. They slung a wicker basket across my shoulder, and I climbed a ladder into a peach tree's canopy. From the treetop I could see the dry desert hillside, upholstered in the tawny elephant hide that housed rattlesnakes, scorpions, sage, and sun-heated rocks. Eden, in a word. I stretched forth my hand. The peach seemed all juice and flesh of amber and gold and garnet, such beauty suited to somewhere heavenly. There was nothing to do but bend forward, caught up in the perfection of the morning, tears and juice running together until both were finished.

≈

The intricacies and richness of South Asian food has held my heart and palate in thrall for decades. At my favourite restaurant, one of the owners greets me at the door, her small brown hands folded together like nesting wrens. "*Salaam alaikum.*" She brings me the ideal antidote to hard work, a cup of spiced chai before I dine: dhal, amber lentils and chickpeas scented with ginger and cumin; alabaster rice; *rogan josh*, many spices smoothed into its mahogany sauce; *aloo gobi*, cauliflower and potatoes turmeric-tinged gold. I pick up my naan, tear off a small piece, fold it between my fingers to pick up my food, feeling close to heaven.

As I lick my fingers, I remember that eating with our hands triggers digestive enzymes in our bellies, but science doesn't whet the appetite. I prefer to think of eating with my hands as a contemplative act, a *mudra*, the divinity of human effort that rises above prayer. Putting my hands on my food reinforces the transformation at the heart of cooking and eating, most especially for me through the warm spices I love—cumin, cloves, coriander, cardamom, cinnamon—flavourings of a world I have never visited but have felt drawn to since I was eighteen and a vegetarian student of limited means, living on Vancouver's Eastside. My side of town was crowded with South Asian shops and restaurants serving affordable suppertime buffets. I learned to fill my soup pot with lentils, basmati, chickpeas, my cup with chai. In hot weather I adopted Indian-style loose cotton salwar and kameez, and draped silk scarves around my neck year-round.

≈

Two days before my birthday, the South Asian restaurant's television—perpetually tuned to CNN—announces the anniversary of the birth of Dr. Martin Luther King, Jr., almost fifty years before mine. The rise and fall of his voice during "I Have a Dream," his most famous speech, delivered at the Lincoln Memorial on 28 August 1963, embellishes my evening meal with the rapture and rhythm of faith. I listen to his lyrical dream of equality, of all peoples gathering at the table, of an end to bias based on race.[1] That night, a tenuous skein of what might be hope, as fragile as the licorice scent of anise seed, ravels itself around my heart.

≈

The narrow Traffic Bridge across the South Saskatchewan River closes, to be replaced with a broader bridge. One winter-white Sunday, demolition explosives flash. The outer arcs of the ancient metal frame cartwheel to the ice below, snapping girders and triangular trusses. Just the central segment is left standing, reduced to disembodied arc and linkage. The struts and cross-rails have little left to suggest a bridge: a steel creel precariously balanced on two concrete pillars mid-stream; what was lit each winter by loops of twinkling lights is now open air cut by curving metal. It haunts me, calls to me on my weekly walks across an adjacent bridge.

Workers worry at the riverbank with buckets and rakes attached to ant-like machinery, the icy water lapping at pylons that hold the span aloft. What about this breakage fascinates me? Its isolation? Its war-zone tenacity and rebirth, despite its essential brokenness? Its role as linkage between here and somewhere—or something—else? An earthbound rainbow, then? Arcs of concrete and iron, a small moment of heaven rendered into prosaic shape, still bearing its history of rapture from beyond?

≈

One winter evening at the restaurant, curry gravy drips to my wrists as I eat. Soon a young Muslim family enters. After the owner's ritual greeting, they take the table beside me. They speak no English, but study me covertly as I watch them—a young boy, his father; his mother in a hijab with a baby in her arms—eat with their hands, too. The boy grabs a chapati and crams it into his mouth, barely chewing between swallows until his father lays his arm across the boy's narrow shoulder and bends to whisper in his ear. The woman glances once at me, and before she touches her dhal and chapati, she opens her clothing to her infant, drapes her shawl over them both and nurses her, the two of them closed off in an existence of their own. She nods to me as they leave an hour later.

Yes—the owner confirms when she brings my chai—the family is Syrian, and yes, they are refugees, among the first to arrive in the city. There's nothing memorable about the event, just another family eating dinner at a table beside a stranger. But the Syrian woman's infinitesimal acknowledgement, and our unity in eating without utensils, her matter-of-fact but private care of her babe, transforms the ordinary into extraordinary. That small family occupies me all the way home, and I recall the intimacy and rapture of nursing my own babies, the memory as enduring as the scent of ginger and cardamom on my hair.

≈

At a poetry workshop, my friend Kathleen brings out a tiny quilt, handmade by her daughter, a representation of farm fields rendered in velvet and silk, embroidery overstitching as barriers, ornate, delicate. Beneath my fingers, the subtle fences and fields leap into life. The quilt sits on the table as we write, defamiliarizing the everyday, stirring memory: my youngest son in a fabric store, blissfully rubbing a piece of velvet between his fingers; myself, cutting and stitching coral silk into a robe I'd wear for thirty years, its kiss against my bare skin, the tactile pleasure of touch elevated into, yes, rapture.

≈

Leaving the restaurant after dinner that evening, the sun sinking into orange ice, the broken bridge like a damaged monument in the tawny light, I suddenly *see* what the bridge symbolizes: the leap into the mystic that I have yearned for since that long-ago moment in the revival tent. Not the bridge's separation, aloof in the river, nor its endurance, but the launch—effortless, ecstatic—from bank to mid-stream to bank beyond.

The idea circles, alighting finally like an angel's feather of scribbles on my notepad. At my desk, I examine those scribbles, transfer that pollen into ink, praying all the while to preserve its simple clarity, to bring the ineffable to the page. As I write, a poem about the Syrian refugee woman begins to crystallize.

≈

At age twelve, I joined the Baptists when I fell desperately in love with my friend Maria's mother, who commanded the Baptist youth group's choir like an avenging angel. For her, I endured sword drill, using Bible as sword: "Swords away!"— my grandmother's worn leather King James Bible tucked under my arm. "Swords drawn!"—raising the Bible like a weapon. "Exodus, chapter 20: 1–17. Charge!" We raced to the page, Bibles jubilant banners when we found the page, then hurried to Matthew 22: 35–40, Mark 12: 28–34. I knew that book like a best friend, the soft folds of its pages, the sleek edges like silk. I knew Moses, returning from the mountain with the stone tablets, and the apostles Matthew and Mark, all using the same language: "Thou shalt not kill." "Love thy neighbour as thyself." Decades later, I see the drawn weapons of extremists' videoed beheadings and Donald Trump's exhortations to build a wall, bricks cemented with non-white blood, as the same ecstatic fervour I felt, stoked to fever pitch. But I don't understand it, rapture transmuted into something ugly and dangerous.

≈

When I visit Kathleen, we spend an evening looking at her handmade quilts, weavings of seemingly random scraps into patterns, their nuanced relationships visible only from a distance, to eyes willing not merely to look, but to *see* patterns and links. I pore over cut, colour, and clarity like an Amsterdam diamond master. When I leave, a book for beginners in hand, I swear to make quilts for my family and friends, for my own walls and bed.

≈

The poem touches down, and I capture the first draft in prose, distill it into line breaks and stanzas, sleep, wake, revise, and walk again past the bridge, gaze wide-eyed at its impermanence and mystery.

≈

Standing in Saskatoon's city council chambers to read one of my poems, I look at fourteen white men in suits behind the table, gather up my breath: "I am pleased to tell you that this poem is about diversity." Council members straighten in their soft chairs. Applause ripples around the room from the Indigenous men and women present to speak their case for truth and reconciliation in a city notorious in its day for cops dragging inebriated Indigenous men into frozen fields and abandoning them. Solidarity is tangible and I weep while reading, bearing witness:

> *The moon above her father's orchard in Damascus*
> *is a peach, ripe for plucking . . .*
> *In the camp on the sand dunes*
> *beside the sea, the moon is a pomegranate, red*
> *with the blood of children . . .*[2]

≈

On the anniversary of the death of Martin Luther King, Jr., the restaurant's television replays the great man's "I've Been to the Mountaintop" speech, given the night before his assassination in Memphis on 4 April 1968. King sounded prescient, as if he knew his days had rolled to their conclusion, speaking of his lack of fear, his happiness at seeing the Promised Land, but the hard fact of not arriving there with his people. Of glory.[3] He crossed the river Jordan into rapture the next day.

≈

I think I am finished with the bridge, the woman, the moon, but they blur together and morph into comets, returning sporadically to remind me of—what? I'm still not sure. Gratitude, I suspect, and appreciation for small things. Small glows of pleasure accrue: a new quilt, half-finished, and a gift of sea-washed silk destined to become my new robe. On hot days, my salwar and kameez. At home in my own kitchen, curry and peach chutney, even though my best jars bear insufficient resemblance to the fresh peach I ate through the valley of my tears. The broken bridge is mended, but the memory still invites my leap without asking how, even as it whispers—*yes!*—to rapture.

SURRENDER
IN IAMBIC
TETRAMETER

Turner sky, sun below the horizon, hinted at what the day might become. Three whitetail deer on the grid road watched my approach. When I was thirty feet away, they ambled into the ditch, leaped the fence, vanished. A moment later, their tails flagged their passage across the hay field. Chickadees and meadowlarks sang pop tunes from the aspens as gravel squelched beneath my runners, my arms metronoming the pace.

The first few kilometres were hard, as they always are. At the sixth, my body settled into a rhythm that ate up the distance, a deliberate 1-2-3-4, equal but alternating stresses. Iambic tetrameter. My mind let go. At ten kilometres, my watch buzzed the distance, an electronic jitterbug of congratulations. At twelve kilometres, then again at thirteen, fifteen, seventeen, my left hip twinged a familiar DEW Line warning.

That was me, spring, summer, fall, winter. It was never about speed; it was about putting one foot in front of the other, over and over. No matter if I ran alone or in a race, my only—my fiercest—competitor was myself.

I've been grounded for months while I attempt to recover from a long-time hip injury. I miss running. Running affords me room to think, a happy by-product for a writer. Dialogues come clear, plot points unravel, poems touch down, essay endings evolve, all while running. Words arrive, not in dribbles, but as gushes—me pregnant again, my water breaking so the life waiting within can become its own self. Walking's relationship to the creative life is well documented. Annie Dillard, William Wordsworth, Virginia Woolf, and others intuitively drew on what scientists at Stanford University studied in 2014: walking increases creativity.[1] Running has the same effect. That's part of why I run. It's arriving at surrender, the grounded state of being that allows creativity to take root. What some runners call the zone.

≈

My practice of running didn't spring from a vacuum. I've been getting physical all my life. Age seven, my first gymkhana. I perched in a saddle aboard Rebel, my mother's old gelding. I kicked him into a canter and he rocking-horsed over the first small jump, the saddle suddenly an uneasy dinghy on rough seas, Rebel's long strides like waves. A second fence, and the waves became tsunamis that shook my boots from the stirrups. At the third, I hung on to the pommel like a life-raft, but it wasn't enough, and I pitched out of the saddle to the ground. What felt like hours passed as I struggled, trying to lift my left boot high above my shoulder to reach the stirrup dangling, elusive, out of reach. Eventually, someone tall strode into the arena, picked me up, brushed me off, and set me back in the saddle.

Soon after, my parents bought me a mount more suited to my height—an Appaloosa pony. We christened him Papoose, a Narragansett Algonquian word for *child*, perfect for my pint-sized polka-dot descendant of a breed whose ancestors had carried the Nimiipuu, the Nez Perce Nation, across the high plateaux of the Pacific Northwest.

That pony detonated my life wide open to include horses. Bareback on Papoose each morning at Rebel's heels as Mom and I took them out to pasture, I felt the first hint of the freedom riding offered. Then one afternoon, partway through my riding lesson, Papoose took the bit in his mouth. He ignored my sawing at the reins and sailed over the four-foot paddock gate at a gallop—à la British cartoonist Norman Thelwell's famous fat-ponies-and-small-girls cartoons—with me on his back, shrieking in an unholy blend of fear and glee as we careened across the road to where Rebel grazed.

On horseback I was happy, even in the *Bleak House*–angst moments no growing kid can escape. Happiness was the indelible smell of horses on my sweaters, horsehair in my pockets, my jeans worn thin by hours in a saddle, my mind rocked by the rhythm of posting—that rise-and-fall of a rider that makes iambic tetrameter out of a trotting horse's footfalls.

≈

My GP sounds an alarm when she reads the results of my bloodwork in the summer of 2016. "Elevated cholesterol, but nothing to be worried about," Dr. T. tells me. "Eat better, exercise more, come back in three months."

O outrage! That I—a chef! a dedicated vegetable lover!—should need to "eat better"! I huff and puff indignantly all the way home. But the truth is in my increased padding and widened girth. So, I choke down my hubris, consult a fitness guru, bring home a running and exercise program. I hang the program on the fridge and faithfully exercise—for about a month. But no sense of urgency attaches itself to the page or to my body, so when I miss first one run and then a second, I quietly let it go, half-guilty, half-relieved. I'm plenty fit, I tell myself. I've been a jock, a chef, a restaurateur. I'm *active*. I have a daily yoga practice. Surely, I can cruise on the muscle memory and goodwill of my body for another year or two.

≈

One afternoon, my parents unloaded a young gelding from the horse trailer. His dappled coat was burnished gold, with black markings and a white blaze from forelock to muzzle. His gait and attitude suggested compressed springs, sparks ready to ignite.

"He's an Arab–Quarter Horse cross. You've outgrown that pony," Dad said as Mom handed me the lead-line. I fell madly in love, and named him Brandy. My tween and teen years would be obsessively spent on his back. Learning how to *really* ride a horse over a big fence. Learning serenity, patience, surrender, the art of friendship. Brandy flung his heart ahead of himself at every stride, and like him, I never met a fence I didn't want to soar over. But bravery doesn't make friends. Dad was in the air force, and we moved every two years: I'd learned that friends were the people you left behind, and an air of "outsider" clung at every new school. Sure, I played tough competitive volleyball and basketball, but neither my killer-instinct spiking nor my high-curve corner shot helped me make friends. Identifying the bond between the physical and the mental worlds would come in my later years, but in school, there was a clear division between the jocks and the brains. I straddled both camps. I was too smart for my own good, too aware of not being like everyone else, too desperate for friends, didn't realize I should keep some opinions to myself. So, although I persisted in trying to fit in at school, Brandy was my best friend.

Every afternoon after school, I'd saddle up. We would sail over fences in our riding ring, alone and helmetless (oh the risk I was taking, unknowing), overseen by the pileated woodpeckers in the arbutus and cedar trees. Or I'd pack an apple and cheese, and we'd jog beside the pipeline threading the hills between the logging road and the Puntledge River. Weekly riding classes and weekend horse shows were group affairs, but daily riding remained a solitary experience, shared only with my horse. His ears, flickering ahead of me as I sat in the saddle, were the defining sight of my teenaged years.

Brandy was a talented jumper, with great arcing action. To their credit, my parents were as keen as I; they paid my entry fees and drove me to weekend horse shows, trundling with the camper and horse trailer up and down Vancouver Island. An old black and white photo in my album shows Mom and me at a small-town show, grinning, our hands full of ribbons and trophies, Brandy on a lead-line at my shoulder. Not until I was a mother, witnessing my sons' sometimes-reckless behaviour, would I comprehend the nail-biting torture I subjected my parents to during those years of jumping: if you jump, you fall. Sprains, strains, dislocations, bandages, tensor bands, crutches—my body endured all manner of physical abuse, and years later, the bill would come due. When I did fall, my parents never complained or chastised; they would unsaddle and stable my horse, then make another trip to emergency to have my wounds bound up.

Over time, I became a more graceful rider when I learned to love dressage (French for *training*), the equestrian equivalent of yoga. At its highest level, dressage is an art form, the "airs above the ground" practised by Olympic competitors, and the white Lipizzaner stallions of Vienna. But even for novices, dressage builds up horse's and rider's fitness and suppleness. You ride around a small arena marked with letters of the alphabet, trying to hit the marks in a memorized series of movements, attempting to become one with your horse. A Zen centaur. It's boring until you arrive in that zone, the moment of surrender.

But combined eventing owned my reckless heart. It's a triple play: dressage; a cross-country gallop over high, sturdy fences in rough country; a placid round of stadium jumping. I discounted dressage's subtlety and control in those days, despite the fact that it often determined the overall winner of the combined event. To me, eventing was all about the cross-country, its requisite speed and bravery. I was dimly aware of but could not express the sheer effrontery of jumping, the curving bascule of a horse's body as it leaves the earth and leaps into the sky. Of release from gravity. Of surrender to the winds of chance and risk, of the inevitability of landing, of sometimes falling. Not that I realized it back then. Back then I was only aware of the simplicity of adrenalin, the addictive attraction of big fences and speed from a horse's back.

≈

In April 2017, almost a year after my GP first raised the alarm, I see my naturopath, Annette.

"Run for your life," she tells me after she studies my irises. "Your arteries are clogging."

I've never understood—but still trust—this voodoo of eyes. How does an iridologist gather such details? Shakespeare wrote about the windows of the eyes revealing the soul in *Richard III*.[2] But eyes reveal the body, as well: iridology assesses the irises' colours, patterns, and structure, which identify corresponding physiological changes in organs and body parts as well as illnesses and infections. Magic, but practical magic.

I've always had a view of my innards along the lines of Henry Ford's Model T, a high-performance engine stripped down to chassis, valves, engine. Suddenly, when Annette invokes cholesterol, my image of my inner pipes morphs to an Edsel, Ford's famous flop, one clogged with black carbon buildup and calcified U-joints, spluttering to a halt or stuttering into explosion. Run, she says, so I research running and pick a goal: I enroll in a 10K trail race to be held in mid-September, on steep bluffs and escarpments overlooking the South Saskatchewan River.

What? Am I crazy? Then I register for a 5K race along Saskatoon's riverbanks. In July. This is April. Really crazy? I can't run out our driveway and back! So, I finally start following that training program that still hangs on the fridge. I run and walk, slowly adding distance along the roads that frame our land, part of the prairie's grid road system, where distances are remarkably easy to measure. As I run, I remember that the grid was imposed on the prairies by the federal government as a colonizing measure in 1869, deliberately disrupting the existing Métis system of lots that provided equal access to the river. The roads I run lie fifteen kilometres from the North Saskatchewan River; with each step, I wonder how I'd measure my life if the lots still ran northward to the banks. Fear drives me at first, then pleasure sets in, and I recognize the 1-2-3-4 count of poetry, of horseback riding.

≈

Brandy and I made the Saskatchewan equestrian team in the 1975 Western Canada Summer Games, for combined eventing. Brandy was a handful while jumping, and one day, Elaine Partington, our coach, said in exasperation, "Dee, sit still! Sit down and clear your mind. Don't telegraph. Soften your wrists and relax your hands on the reins. Be calm, and he will be." I breathed in and willed myself to calm. To my utter surprise,

Brandy settled. Instead of his normal high-headed charge, he cantered quietly to the fence and popped over, no fuss, no drama. The lesson stuck: as long as I stayed calm, Brandy stayed calm. That reframing of my mental posture, coupled with dressage's refinement of my physical posture, reinvented my abilities as a rider. For years I had dreamed of riding on the Canadian Olympic equestrian team. That summer, for several shining months, my ambitions and my abilities aligned. But I forgot how empathetic horses are.

≈

My first race—the 5K—arrives. Novice that I am, I start faster than my normal pace, and the middle kilometres stretch out like lost country roads. I'm exhausted when I cross the finish line, but ecstatic to collect the first medal I've earned since my equestrian days. I add strengthening exercises to my yoga repertoire, and soon my sister in Toronto is commenting on photographs that reveal what she calls "your gorgeous arms laced with muscles." I feel ready.

I am. The 10K racetrack is carved into hillsides and coulees, and I, like all the other runners, slow to a walk at the steepest points along the narrow goat trails. Each time I emerge at the top of one of the linked ridges, the wind nearly blows me off my feet. Running down rock-and-mud-caked slopes, I quickly learn to jump sideways and forward from one foot to the other, exhilarating and brash, like a skier carving a steep descent. On a long downward incline just past the halfway marker, and again in the final kilometre, I open the jets, mind humming, revelling in my body's ability to gas up and go. Two hundred metres from the finish line, I trip and fall flat on my face, rip open one knee on an errant stone. I'm cursing and laughing when I get up, and I finish the race at a gallop, strong, smiling, amazed.

≈

At the Summer Games, Brandy and I waited at the starting line of the cross-country course. It was a blustery grey morning, and the anxiety in my gut churned into a storm. My coach Elaine's gloved hand on my knee felt like a ten-ton weight. "Be brave," she said. Seconds later, the starting gun sounded, and I kicked Brandy into a canter.

The first fences were simple—a brush fence, a stone wall, a wagon, a gate, all invitations to the dance. I could imagine Elaine: "Breathe!" she'd say. "Sit down. Let go!" My breath started to unravel from its clenched pose in my ribcage.

Eight fences in, we cantered down a slight slope toward a small post-and-rail that concealed a drop landing on the far side. Ordinarily fearless Brandy dug in his toes and stopped dead. Aghast, I pulled him around, the clock in my brain pounding like my telltale heart, time lost as I repositioned him for a second approach. Another refusal, so abrupt it nearly put me over his head. Then a third. Our clock stopped. We were eliminated, disgraced, forced to retire and walk off the course. Brandy's reins clenched in my cold fingers, I cried bitterly on Elaine's shoulder when my last teammate crossed the finish line.

Eventually I realized that I alone was responsible for Brandy's refusals, just as my nervous energy had been responsible for him rushing his fences. The small drop jump was just the precursor: halfway through walking the course the day before the competition, I had choked with fear as we stopped at a rail fence perched on the lip of a steep fall-away path down into an old quarry. My coach talked about lines of approach, and strategies for landing, but I didn't hear a word as I looked into the abyss. How could we land safely? Where? I'd known then that I couldn't do it, and the next day Brandy read my response.

A year later I left Brandy behind when I moved to Vancouver. For a while, I rode the bus to an equestrian centre in Langley, where the manager was grateful to have an experienced rider exercise some of the owner's expensive jumpers. But the place felt too high-toned for me, all white fences enclosing lush paddocks. I had grown accustomed to the prairie's scrubby sand hills and weathered-barnboard make-do pragmatism. And none of the horses was mine. All stood well over sixteen hands, far taller than my half-jigger of Brandy, who, at fifteen hands, had been practically a pony in the warm-blooded world of jumpers. I conflated those elegant horses into one super-horse and convinced myself that it was all too much for short-legged country-mouse-me.

≈

I see my GP again. "Your cholesterol is still high," she says severely. "I'll refer you to the specialist. Resign yourself to life on statins."

No way. I don't like the sound of the side effects of the statins that manage cholesterol. Statins inhibit production of an enzyme needed to produce cholesterol; that enzyme's absence causes severe muscle pain and memory loss. I'm fond of my wits and my hard-earned muscles. So, I decide to eat more beans instead. I was a vegetarian for thirteen years, as a student cook in Vancouver, and then in carnivore Calgary. To this day, I love India's sophisticated meatless dishes, so it's no effort to eat more beans, lentils, chickpeas. Comfortably settled in my new diet, I set my sights on running a half-marathon, twenty-one kilometres, and begin training.

≈

I enrolled in cooking school in Vancouver in 1981 as part of a federal government program to enlist more women in the trades, my only riding the rare hop aboard Brandy when I'd visit my parents on the farm. My mother reported his death at twenty-seven, and my love affair with horses came to a sliding stop. Horse-owning friends who knew my history lent me saddles and I mounted up occasionally, but both muscle memory and emotional bond had dwindled. My Olympic dream was extinguished. I told myself I'd been born into a working-class family, that competitive riding was a rich woman's game. It may have been true, but I never forgot that moment when Brandy's toes had dug in, when my empathetic horse cold-read my innermost feeling of dread.

Over the years as a chef, I flexed my culinary muscles. Standing in my miniscule restaurant kitchen with my kids in the nineties, we read a review that described my food as having good qi (Chinese for *life-energy* or *flow*), bursting with layered flavours and *umami*, that near-mystical fifth taste of savouriness. My sons looked down at the curry on their plates. Their everyday fare, seasoned with cumin, coriander, cardamom, cinnamon, cloves.

"Tasty," one said.

"Don't use that word, Mom hates it," said the other.

My restaurant lasted two years. Two years of living chest-deep in the river of inspiration, immersed in that sense of surrender into the flow. Then my body burnt out, my sons moped for my presence, and we sold the restaurant. I began to write. About food.

More years. Turning fifty wasn't hard. In my late fifties, though, my body began to betray me. Weight gain contributed to a hiatal hernia. Some foods turned my innards into an acid bath. I gave up coffee, then wine, took to eating ginger and drinking ginger tea as lullabies to my racketing gut. Then osteoarthritis invaded my hands and feet, knees and hips, partial payment on high-interest damage done in my teenaged years. Wafers of emptiness showed up on a bone scan: osteoporosis. Then I came closer to sixty. How to face up to a number that *sounds* old? Especially when the face looking back at me has aged noticeably, any vestiges of pretty ironed out by living. Wrinkles where they haven't been before. Plum-stains under my eyes. Hair stuck on the "dull" setting, eyebrows disappearing from the ground up. Sister Age has tiptoed up behind me, tapped my shoulder, and now looks at me from my mirror. Fewer years remain than I've lived. How to do all I still want to accomplish? What does the clock's louder ticking mean? Will I ever finish my first novel? Write more than one?

The complication is that I changed careers, jumped ship as a chef for love of the literature I dreamed of writing. *Lit-Tra-Chure*. Time keeps ticking inexorably on. And me, finally realizing that writing is a slow ship beset by bailing and tacking and loss of wind in the sails. What if my arcs of ability and desire never intersect, a sorry replay of my equestrian history? If I took up writing too late to become as good as I want to be? The fear of unfulfilled ambition, that dull area, the doldrums where dreams founder, is where I find myself as sixty eases closer. Depression rolls in. I avoid people. Find reasons to stay home. Defer celebrating anything.

The New Year turns. My birthday arrives, and when I wake, I'm sixty—but still me. Still breathing, still running. Still writing. It's a relief to surrender into the realization that I can only write what I can write. The optimism that had ebbed floods back. If we are good, and lucky, if our work matches the unpredictable dots and dashes of the current zeitgeist, we may be published. Some of us—a very few—win awards. But there are no medals for completing the Lit-Tra-Chure life-studies program as there are for finishing a footrace. It's all about loving the process of writing, one foot in front of the other, the same flow as running and riding.

Eventually a recurring hip flare-up signals the long-delayed balance owing finally threatening to come due. Sitting in the physiotherapist's office, I wonder about my decisions, a whole string of them, stretching back my entire life. Should I have found another horse after Brandy died? Pursued my Olympic dream? Stayed in Vancouver after cooking school? Stayed in cooking after selling my restaurant? Stayed with food writing instead of moving on to write Lit-Tra-Chure? But debating "right" or "not right" is a mug's game: these are the choices I made. What I *can* do is do right by them. So I've given up watching televised chef shows: they remind me too acutely of what I chose to give up, and what I'll never become. And I have embraced the reality that I, like M.F.K. Fisher, am a food writer, in addition to whatever else I choose to write.

My choices still bedevil me. Maybe they always will. The distance between the physical and intellectual still gives me pause. Trust in creative flow comes hard, seasoned with doubts. My response is another surrender: I will keep writing what I am able to write, nurtured by my running practice, what I feed myself, and my loved ones.

I run the half-marathon in Vancouver, then a half-marathon trail race—a return to Saskatchewan Landing's steep slopes, where I tested myself with my first 10K race. A trio of half-marathons, a flurry of 10Ks. Then another stutter: the hip problem escalates, and I am grounded. No running. Just the small, deliberate movements of physiotherapy. I face months, maybe longer, of near-inactivity while we retrain my body, with no choice but surrender. Running and jumping have brought me a long way. Writing may have to take me the final kilometres. But the rhythm is the same, the swinging 1-2-3-4 of iambic tetrameter of horses' hooves and runners' footfalls. And poetry.

THE LAKE,
LEAVING

I'm wearing my winter gear—fur-lined hat with balaclava beneath it, snow pants, long coat, heavy Sorels, and fuzzy mitts—when Jake and I stop halfway down the driveway on our morning constitutional. He's a young golden retriever, not a type A dog at all, and he looks at me for permission, then at my nod and without barking, he galumphs through the snow among the aspens, stopping often to shovel his nose through the snow. He comes up grinning, snow falling from his whiskers, then pivots and takes off again. The trees are bleached almost white for several feet from the ground up, lasting residue of the floodwaters they stood in for seven years. They've rotted through, I know, but the grove is still home to chickadees, juncos, nuthatches, larks, and at least one magpie couple's mess of a nest still sprawls over the branches of the tallest tree. It's the same tree where I've observed hawks, ravens, even a juvenile bald eagle. The wind is primal, and I turn my back to the north so it rips past without effect.

A month ago, the driveway was lined with willow shrubs that last year caught the snow, snow that drifted into impenetrable dunes, locking us into the yard in a way I'd foreseen years ago when the lake first arrived, but it was the lake I'd imagined as culprit, not the surrounding willow greens that would spring up. These past months, driven by the spectre of soon-flying snow, my son Darl, Dallas, his partner of the last five years, and I spent arduous hours and weeks cutting down those willows, heaping them at the bottom of the driveway that serves as causeway. Today, the snow blows freely, unimpeded. I wish the wind would track its load of snow all the way south to Mexico.

≈

For seven years, we were neighbours with shorebirds, water birds, muskrats, dragonflies. We suddenly lived in paradise. On my daily walks, I learned to identify a dozen species of waterfowl, among them grebes, coots, canvasbacks, teals, pintails, buffleheads, ruddy ducks, and mergansers; and shorebirds that included avocets and killdeer by the dozen.

One day, a blue heron showed up, her angle-iron wings and legs almost invisible in the cattails where she stood for hours, patiently hunting. What was she hunting? Our curiosity led us to Trevor Herriot, a Saskatchewan naturalist.

"Fish!" he said. "All those birds who've come to call have likely carried in fish eggs on their feet."

Another week, a brown pelican did a flyby in slow motion, her billowing wings scooping air from the sky. Canada geese nested by the multitude, leaving ash-like green shit on the driveway where they daily crossed over from one part of the lake to the other.

≈

When winter rolled in across the lake's first year of existence, we looked on the icy expanse surrounding our home, and we planned a bonspiel.

This greeting of the sublimely inalterable, making it welcome, surrendering, became the only reasonable response. Surrender is more graceful than giving up, less adrenalin-laced than going to futile war. Surrender allows you to raise your head and assess the situation, then look your oppressor in the eye. In his sermons collected in *Strength to Love*, Martin Luther King, Jr. speaks of faith, endurance, patience, determination.[1]

Of course, King was talking about a people surviving a flood of hatred, not a farm surviving a flood of water, but the lesson holds. You can't fight Mother Nature, but you can outwait—and maybe outwit—her. So that winter, under a vast arc of endless blue bordering on infinity, we filled vinegar jugs with water to use as our curling rocks. We marked concentric rings and a central "button" with red food colouring, alerted the Rural Municipality that we'd be setting a fire, set a match to paper and kindling on the verge of the lake, appointed a fire-minder, heated cider. The wind blew vast swatches of the ice free of snow, and looking down, you could see fragments of aspen boughs trapped in the crystalline ice, and leaves in layers like a mosaic. A few people brought skates and twirled for hours on an expanse that an Olympic athlete would have envied. Others strapped on skis or snowshoes and made their way around the perimeter of the lake to the fields beyond. Our dogs played, too, pursuing errant rocks, nosing them back to the sidelines or carrying them off as trophies, chasing the brooms of the sweepers who polished the path for the slowing rocks. That afternoon, Peter Stoicheff, at the time the University of Saskatchewan's dean of Arts and Sciences (and currently its president), lay down on the ice to serve as a "human hack" for the curlers who were struggling with the slippery ice. The dogs didn't know what to make of that.

When our hands got cold, we ceded the rink to the wildlife and went indoors. What else to do? I'd made bread and chili. Our friends brought pies, salads, squares, tortillas, cookies, chocolates, wine, bourbon, and high spirits. Fifty friends filled our kitchen and living room. We filled our bowls and glasses and held up winter as a toast.

The Dogpatch bonspiel was only possible because of the lake. We'd go on to host an outdoor bonspiel each New Year's Day for seven years.

≈

It took eighteen months to complete, but eventually, in an amazing feat of winter engineering, the driveway was built up into a causeway, with front-end loaders breaking through metre-thick ice to build the foundation. A berm went up around the house, as well, burying my grandmother's old well-tended garden beneath its protective shoulders. We built raised beds to replace it.

Our dog Amigo, inherited when my parents moved to town, hunted the muskrats who swam the lake, but the lake nearly got him in the end. One winter, as we drove home from a trip to a book festival in Montana, our friend Philip called. He and his partner Yvette were house-and-dog-sitting for us. Amigo was trapped in ice and mud along the lakeside, he said. They were engineering a bridge out of old tires and two-by-sixes to evacuate him.

It was a brave—and foolishly risky—act. Old Amigo was a Great Pyrenees. He weighed about 150 pounds and had grown rank with age and whatever joint pains he couldn't tell us about. He bit people—including me, whom he loved—on rare occasions when he felt trapped or insecure. It was cold and the pair of them spent hours outside, rescuing that old dog. When we got home, we hauled Amigo onto a blanket and into a wagon that the tractor could tow. We took him to the heated garage in Ken and Sharon's yard, where he and I shivered through the night. The vet's visit the next day pronounced the old dog fit to carry on for a while yet, so we brought him safely home.

≈

In 2017, wet summers were replaced by drought. The water table dropped. In 2018, although melting snow briefly raised the water table again, by spring the lake receded to slough status, two separate puddles of water. The cattails and bulrushes retreated, as well, and the black snails vanished. We watched the water level drop on the frames of two Dodge Model A's in the meadow south of the house. My brother Brad started hauling old cars out as the mud dried into concrete. The pole barn's poles rotted and gave out, and it slowly began to cant to the south; the entire huge building where I'd ridden my horse Brandy over schooling fences in high winter during the mid-seventies slid into what water remained. A year later, when the field dried, we would see a huge front-end loader fitted with a tri-pointed claw pull hundreds of dead cars from the field and deposit them into a score of metal waste boxes before they were hauled away. The pole barn would continue its slow arcing dance with gravity until it toppled.

I began to consider how to reclaim the land where the water had lain for years. Seed it to alfalfa and turn the crop under? Mow its crop of weeds regularly? Spend thousands on new fencing and invite Ken to bring back his cattle to graze? We have no answers yet.

Many people, when they learned of the lake's pending demise, immediately said, "Oh, I bet you can't wait for it to go!" But that isn't the case.

Dave in particular is mourning the passing of the lake. It covered upward of twenty-five acres at its peak, in fact a large slough, but *lake* dignified what was a difficult situation. And now he mourns its loss.

The lake added charm and an element of whimsy to what is otherwise a derelict old farm. And a layer of life—those birds and shore-and-water creatures—that we felt privileged to live beside.

We were forewarned. Within weeks of the lake's arrival, I had called Trevor. "Lakes come and go on the prairie," he said. "In eight or ten years, it'll be gone again."

Sure enough, it's gone. On 2018's final day, I did not mark the rings and set out the firewood. I didn't make the chili and bake sourdough bread. We weren't able to look the frozen lake in the eye. But the raised beds we built after the garden drowned have borne a wondrous crop each year, and the bonspiel became a memory of a mark-your-calendar event. We'll reinvent it in some other form.

POSTSCRIPT

I was born on my dad's twenty-second birthday while he and my mom lived in northeastern France. My dad was in the Royal Canadian Air Force, and at the time he was stationed at the fighter jet station called 2 Wing, near St. Avold. Mom and Dad waited for many months for Dad's very junior seniority to improve enough to allow them a house on the PMQs, or personnel married quarters, on the base. Meanwhile, they lived in the small French town of Berig. Mom spoke German, which was helpful in the district of Alsace-Lorraine—the area had changed hands multiple times, passing from French to German possession and back as wars and their victors determined the area's newest allegiance. By the time my parents arrived in the late 1950s, the region was again French, after being returned to France after the end of the Second World War. But both French and a German dialect called Alsatian were spoken by most residents, and the area's cuisine had a distinctly Germanic flavour that underlaid the French sensibility of fresh, local, and seasonal.

"Once a week a van came through the town, delivering a full case of wine, picking up the empty case, at every house,"

Mom recalls. "The wine was from the Moselle district, famous for its whites. Another van came regularly, too, with smoked and cured pork sausages—like salami—never fresh. Cattle were too valuable to be eaten—I remember seeing oxen in the fields, pulling ploughs. We got frozen chicken—flown in from Canada, probably, because England was still pretty strictly rationed back then—at the PX (the post exchange) on the base. But we bought our fruits and vegetables 'on the economy' (air force slang for the local shops) at the Friday night street market. It was lit by gaslight, and was very pretty—eggplants and peppers and spuds all in stacks, and bunches of fresh herbs."

Dad was often away on training exercises in Sardinia, and Mom, who would have three small children by the time they returned to Canada, made friends with the locals. Their landlord made schnapps from the local yellow Mirabelle plums, and Mom would receive a small glass of schnapps each time she went downstairs to pay the rent. She recalls that local women drank it with a sugar cube between their teeth, but the men took it straight up. At the pub she would often see the publican's son, age twelve, holding a glass of wine and smoking, his big dog lounging on the floor at his feet. She remembers one evening at a birthday celebration, a group of workmen in heavy boots occupied the booth across from them in a café, a big pot of soup on their table. When Dad popped the cork from the Alsatian *crémant* he was opening, the cork flew and landed in their soup. Laughter ensued.

By now you are wondering—why this particular trail of memories? Memories are what remain of my father, who unexpectedly and suddenly passed away in October 2019. I served two kinds of soup at his wake, when my husband, Dave, lifted a glass of schnapps as he offered a toast to Dad's memory. My joint birthday with Dad's this month is my first in my life without him. I miss him. So, here's a toast to fathers everywhere. I hope the cork lands in your neighbour's soup pot.

NOTES

INTRODUCTION

1   M.F.K. Fisher, *The Gastronomical Me: The Art of Eating: 50th Anniversary Edition* (Hoboken: Wiley Publishing, 1990), 353.

LEARNING TO COOK

1   Madeleine Kamman, *The New Making of a Cook: The Art, Techniques and Science of Good Cooking* (New York: William Morrow, 1997), v.

2   Kamman, 15.

3   Kamman, 777.

4   Madeleine Kamman, *When French Women Cook* (New York: Atheneum, 1982), viii.

5   Molly O'Neill, "For Madeleine Kamman, a Gentler Simmer," *New York Times*, 14 January 1998, https://www.nytimes.com/1998/01/14/dining/for-madeleine-kamman-a-gentler-simmer.html.

6   Kamman, *New Making*, 247.

7   O'Neill, "For Madeleine Kamman."

WATERSHED

1   Elizabeth Philips, "Before," in *Torch River* (London, ON: Brick Books, 2007), 15.

PRAIRIE PRAGMATIC

1   Jean Anthelme Brillat-Savarin, *The Physiology of Taste: Or Meditations on Transcendental Gastronomy*, translated with annotations by M.F.K. Fisher (San Francisco: Arion Press, 1994), 16.

WHALE WATCHING

1   "Ripple Rock (Seymour Narrows)," VI-Wilds: Vancouver Island Wilderness and Historical Conservation, accessed 2 February 2021, http://www.geog.uvic.ca/viwilds/ul-ripplerock.html.

2   Dr. George Leonard on *Quirks and Quarks*, CBC Radio, produced by Jim Handman, Jim Lebans, and Mark Crawley, 19 June 2010.

SLOW DOWN, DAMMIT

1   William Blake quoted in Maria Popova, "William Blake's Most Beautiful Letter: A Searing Defense of the Mind and the Creative Spirit," Brain Pickings, 14 July 2016, https://www.brainpickings.org/2016/07/14/william-blake-john-trusler-letter/.

2   Charles Reznikoff, "19," *Five Groups of Verse 1927*, in *The Poems of Charles Reznikoff: 1918–1975*, edited by Seamus Cooney (Jaffrey, NH: Black Sparrow Books, 2005), 73. Copyright © 2005 by The Estate of Charles Reznikoff. Reprinted with the permission of The Permissions Company, LLC on behalf of Black Sparrow / David R Godine, Publisher, Inc., www.godine.com.

THE SPIRAL TUNNELS

1   E.J. Hart, *The Selling of Canada: The CPR and the Beginnings of Canadian Tourism* (Banff, AB: Altitude Publishing, 1983), 7.

2   Pierre Berton and Janet Berton, *Pierre & Janet Berton's Canadian Food Guide* (Toronto: McClelland and Stewart, 1974), 41.

WIEBO'S WAY

1   Josh Ludwig quoted in Colman Byfield, "Wiebo Ludwig's Family Admits to Nothing," *Edmonton Journal*, 17 August 2013, https://

edmontonsun.com/2013/08/17/weibo-ludwigs-family-admits-to-nothing-apologizes-for-nothing-but-says-acts-of-sabotage-in-alberta-were-justified.

2   Jane Ellen Stevens, "Addiction Doc Says: It's Not the Drugs," Aces Too High, 2 May 2017, https://acestoohigh.com/?s=ritualized+compulsive+comfort-seeking&submit=Search.

3   Harmony Ludwig Schilthuis quoted in Byfield, "Wiebo Ludwig's Family."

4   Andrew Nikiforuk, "The Death of the Reverend," *The Tyee*, 11 April 2012, https://thetyee.ca/Opinion/2012/04/11/Wiebo-Ludwig-Obituary/.

RAPTURE

1   Martin Luther King, Jr., "I Have a Dream [28 August 1963]," American Rhetoric, Top 100 Speeches, accessed January 28, 2021, https://www.americanrhetoric.com/speeches/mlkihaveadream.htm.

2   dee Hobsbawn-Smith, "Oranges & Pomegranates 2," *The New Quarterly*, no. 144 (October 2017): 45.

3   Martin Luther King, Jr., "I've Been to the Mountaintop [3 April 1968]," American Rhetoric: Top 100 Speeches, accessed January 28, 2021, https://www.americanrhetoric.com/speeches/mlkivebeentothemountaintop.htm.

SURRENDER IN IAMBIC TETRAMETER

1   May Wong, "Stanford Study Finds Walking Improves Creativity," *Stanford News*, 24 April 2014, https://news.stanford.edu/2014/04/24/walking-vs-sitting-042414/.

2   William Shakespeare, *King Richard III*, in *Complete Works of Shakespeare*, edited by Peter Alexander (London: Collins, 1951), 5.3, 117. References are to act, scene, and line.

THE LAKE, LEAVING

1   Martin Luther King, Jr., "The Ultimate Measure of a Man," in *Strength to Love* (New York: Harper and Row, 1963).

ACKNOWLEDGEMENTS

I acknowledge that I am a guest on Treaty 6 Territory, home of the Cree, Lakoda, Nakoda, and Dene, and the traditional Homeland of the Métis Nation. I pay my respects to the First Nations and Métis ancestors of this place and reaffirm our relationship with one another and with the land, waters, skies, and animals.

Thank you to the Saskatchewan Writers Guild for its ongoing support of Saskatchewan writers, in particular with its retreats and the John V. Hicks Long Manuscript contest, both of which have seen the gestation of many manuscripts into books—including this one. Some of these essays in earlier versions were part of the manuscript that was awarded second prize for the 2014 John V. Hicks Long Manuscript Award.

Thank you to the publishers and editors of the following magazines, newspapers, literary journals, and anthologies where early versions of the following essays have previously appeared:

Creative Nonfiction, Issue 68, Fall 2018: "Cooking for James."

Gastronomica: The Journal of Food & Culture, 2013: "Learning to Cook."

City Palate: The Flavours of Calgary's Food Scene, 2008–09: "Prairie Pragmatic, Parts I, II, II & IV" appear here as "Prairie Pragmatic."

West, 2012, and *City Palate*, 2010: "Whale Watching" and "Fissues" appear here conflated as "Whale Watching."

City Palate, 2009: "Slow Down, Dammit."

City Palate, 1994, and *Calgary Herald*, 2005: "Love Affair with a Wolf" and "Ode to an Oven" appear together here as "Love Affair with a Wolf."

Swerve, 2005: "Shell Games."

Northwest Palate, 2007: "The View From the Vestibule" appears in this book as "The Spiral Tunnels."

Calgary Herald, 2008: "Annual Canning Bee."

untethered magazine, 2015: "Floodplain."

Swerve, 2005: "Feed the Cook" appears in this book as "The Pleasure of Your Company."

Grain, 2014: "Prodigal."

Nomfiction: A Nonfiction Anthology About Food, 2016: "Handmade."

Grainews, 2018: "Chili to Feed a Crowd" and "Why Not Pickle Some of Those Garden Veggies?" appear together and enlarged as "The Lake, Leaving."

Grainews, 2020: "Shared Memories" appears as "Postscript" in this book, and a version of "M.F.K. Fisher and Me" appears as the preface of this book.

More than a decade after my essay "Almost Perfect" appeared in *Western Living* in 2007, I took a second look at the life of Wiebo Ludwig, resulting in a new piece, "Wiebo's Way." "Wiebo's Way" appeared in *Prairie Fire*, summer 2019, after it won the 2018 Prairie Fire Press and McNally Robinson

Booksellers Creative Non-fiction Writing Contest. Thank you to *Prairie Fire*, and to judge Myrna Kostash.
"Watershed" was awarded an honourable mention in *The New Quarterly*'s Edna Staebler Personal Essay Contest, 2013.

≈

A book needs a village to support its birth. Among those I need to thank: years ago I was blessed with wise coaches who identified what I had only guessed at—a mercurial dreamer's spark that would see me restless from job to job and home to home until I found myself as a writer. Thank you, Lori Marcoux and Phil Holcomb of Extraordinary Learning/21st Century Leadership.

A heartfelt note of remembrance of my late culinary coaches, who were friends and colleagues as well as inspirations. I first met Anita Stewart in 1993, in Cuisine Canada, and we traded ideas, books, and hugs whenever our paths across Canada coincided. When I was redefining my life after Dave and I moved to Saskatchewan, Anita encouraged me in my decision to return to university in my fifties. Madeleine Kamman, whom I first met in 1985 in France, offered invaluable guidance in 1992 when we visited her at Beringer Vineyards in the Napa Valley, where she was running the School for American Chefs. When I wrote to her in despair after my then-husband and I sold our restaurant, Foodsmith, in 1994, she urged me to remember all that I had learned about food and cooking, and suggested that I write and teach. I remember Madeleine and Anita with love and gratitude. We do indeed stand on the shoulders of giants.

Thank you to the fine writers who have inspired and taught me the bones of good writing in several disciplines (the boundaries between writing forms are elusive, if not non-existent): Guy Vanderhaeghe, Maureen Scott Harris,

Tim Lilburn, Liz Philips, phil hall, Sue Goyette, David Carpenter, Barry Dempster, Don McKay, Hilary Clark, and Miriam Toews. It's no accident that many of this group are poets.

Thank you to the inimitable Jeanette Lynes, writer and director of the MFA in Writing program at the University of Saskatchewan, under whose watch two of these essays came to life, and to my colleagues in the MFA program for their insights that made the work better—Sarah Taggart, Mika Lafond, Elise Godfrey, James Pepler, and Sheila Janzen.

And thank you to the members of my writing group, Visible Ink—Lisa Bird-Wilson, Rita Bouvier, Murray Lindsay, Andréa Ledding, Gayle Smith, and Regine Haensel—for many years of support, sharp eyes, on-point comments, friendship and camaraderie, and of course, food and drink.

My heartfelt thanks to the Saskatchewan—and Canadian!—writing and arts community, who have welcomed me as a friend and valued colleague.

Thank you to my darling friends who feed me in so many ways, among them Sarah-jane Newman, Phyllis McCord, Sharon Osborne, Amy Jo Ehman, Gail Norton, Karen Anderson, Jenn Cockrall-King, Jenn Sharp, Madhur Anand, Rosemary Griebel, Roy Hinchey, Kathleen Wall, Shon Profit, Jenni Lessard, Noelle Chorney, Micheline Maylor-Kovitz, Vijay Kachru, Catherine Hortsing, Angeline Schellenberg, and Cathy Ostlere. I am blessed to have such a long list, and send love to those not listed, especially "my" farmers.

Thank you to my family, who endure my obsessions with grace and good will, and to my sister Lee and my mom in particular, for sharing our family history with me when such things finally became relevant to me and my life. And a note of appreciation for our dog, Jake, who anticipates our long daily thinking-time walks and runs with joy, and shares them with enthusiasm.

Thank you to my publisher, University of Regina Press, and the entire team, especially copy editor, Kendra Ward; acquisitions editor, Daniel Lockhart; cover designer, Duncan Campbell; managing editor, Kelly Laycock; director, Kris Luecker; and proofreader, Candida Hadley. *Milles mercis* to the marketing team at ZG—Zoe Grams, Ariel Hudnall, and Sarah Dunn—for stellar work; and to photographer Richard Marjan, for making the most of my gently aging face in midwinter light. My thanks also to all those whose efforts behind the scenes contributed to the betterment of this book. My humility and gratitude for seeing the worth of this work and helping me polish it.

Thank you to SK Arts for financial support that allowed me to concentrate on writing *Bread & Water*.

And finally, to my husband Dave Margoshes, all love and grace and joy and happiness, for being my first reader, my first editor, my last word (well, no, not really!), and for sharing everything with me.

AUTHOR PHOTO BY RICHARD MARJAN

dee Hobsbawn-Smith's writing is often influenced by her history as a chef, restaurateur, caterer, and Slow Food activist. After twenty-seven years in Calgary, Alberta, she now lives on family land west of Saskatoon, Saskatchewan, with her husband, writer Dave Margoshes. Her poetry, essays, short fiction, and journalism have appeared in Canadian, American, and Scottish anthologies, literary journals, websites, newspapers, and magazines. Her book *Foodshed: An Edible Alberta Alphabet* won third prize in Les Dames D'Escoffier's M.F.K. Fisher Award for Excellence in Culinary Writing; Best Culinary Book, High Plains Book Awards; and Best Food Literature Book in Canada (English-language), Gourmand World Cookbook Awards. She earned her MFA in Writing and her MA in English at the University of Saskatchewan. Recent work has appeared in *Creative Nonfiction, Canadian Literature, Queen's Quarterly, The Antigonish Review,* and *The New Quarterly. Bread & Water* is her eighth book. www.deehobsbawnsmith.com

DIGESTIONS

Publishing established and emerging scholars and writers,
DIGESTIONS is a book series that considers the history of food,
the culture of food, and the politics of what we eat from
both a Canadian and a global perspective.

OTHER BOOKS IN THE DIGESTIONS SERIES:

*Uncertain Harvest: The Future of Food
on a Warming Planet*
by Ian Mosby, Sarah Rotz, and Evan D.G. Fraser

Speaking in Cod Tongues: A Canadian Culinary Journey
by Lenore Newman

Arab Cooking on a Prairie Homestead
by Habeeb Salloum

SERIES EDITOR
Lenore Newman
author of *Speaking in Cod Tongues: A Canadian Culinary Journey* and
Lost Feast: Culinary Extinction and the Future of Food
and Canada Research Chair in Food Security and Environment at
University of the Fraser Valley

FOR MORE INFORMATION ABOUT
PUBLISHING IN THE SERIES, PLEASE CONTACT:
Karen May Clark, Acquisitions Editor
University of Regina Press
3737 Wascana Parkway
Regina, Saskatchewan S4S 0A2 Canada
karen.clark@uregina.ca
www.uofrpress.ca